The Silent Child

The Silent Child

Exploring the World of Children
Who Do Not Speak

LAURENT DANON-BOILEAU

translated from the French
by
KEVIN WINDLE

OXFORD
UNIVERSITY PRESS

OXFORD
UNIVERSITY PRESS

Great Clarendon Street, Oxford OX2 6DP

Oxford University Press is a department of the University of Oxford.
It furthers the University's objective of excellence in research, scholarship,
and education by publishing worldwide in

Oxford New York

Athens Auckland Bangkok Bogotá Buenos Aires Cape Town
Chennai Dar es Salaam Delhi Florence Hong Kong Istanbul Karachi
Kolkata Kuala Lumpur Madrid Melbourne Mexico City Mumbai
Nairobi Paris São Paulo Shanghai Singapore Taipei Tokyo Toronto Warsaw

and associated companies in Berlin Ibadan

Published in the United States
by Oxford University Press Inc., New York

English translation © Oxford University Press 2001

This translation is published with the support
of the French Ministry of Culture – *Centre national du livre*.

Originally published in French as *L'Enfant Qui Ne Disait Rien*
© Calmann-Levy 1995

British Library Cataloguing in Publication Data

Data available

Library of Congress Cataloging in Publication Data

Data applied for

ISBN 0–19–823786–3

1 3 5 7 9 10 8 6 4 2

Typeset by Peter Kahrel
Printed in Great Britain
on acid-free paper by
Biddles Ltd.
Guildford and King's Lynn

Contents

Acknowledgements

My thanks are due to all those who lent their help and support in my work with the children and in preparing and drafting the final text in French and its English translation: Dr J. Angelergues, M.-F. Bresson, Dr M. Caron, Dr D. Diatkine, Prof. R. Diatkine, M. Garboua, E. Guened, M. C. Lacombat, Dr G. Lucas, Dr M. Ody, Dr Y. Manella, A. Maupas, A. Morgenstern, V. Picchi, I. Seguin, M. Van Wayenberghe, E. Vialeton, Dr K. Windle.

Responsibility for all errors rests with me.

L.D.-B.

December 2000

The author can be contacted at the following email address: danon@cxt.jussieu.fr

Translator's Note

The English translation has been made in close collaboration with the author, who made small revisions to the text while the work was in progress. The translated version does not, therefore, correspond in every detail to the French version published by Calmann-Lévy in 1995. I am grateful to Laurent Danon-Boileau for his close interest in the translation and his willingness to help with points that caused difficulties for me.

I owe a debt of gratitude to my friend and colleague James Grieve, a highly experienced translator of French literature and until recently a Reader in French at the Australian National University. His encyclopedic knowledge of French and his readiness to spend much time vetting my work have done much to make this a better version than it would otherwise have been. I am also grateful to Jacqueline Mayrhofer, who provided most valuable information about French children's games.

K.W.

Introduction

For fifteen years I've been working with silent children. Generally, when I see them for the first time, they are 3 to 7 years old. Why they cannot speak is a difficult question to answer, although their pathology often bears a resemblance to the symptoms of adult aphasia and childhood autism. In spite of their difficulties, a good many of these children manage to speak after three years of special training. Why is this so? The aim of this book is to find out. I explore the cases of six children through accounts based on notes taken on the day of their sessions. In my view the clinical events that one comes across, even those that at first sight seem trivial,

shed stunning light on the ways in which a child can work his
or her way to language. When I say language, I mean not only
grammar and vocabulary, but also the very special type of human
bond that only language can provide. Some people, such as Jerome
Bruner, refer to this simply as human culture.

In their very first months at school, children are expected to be
able to speak to people they are meeting for the very first time.
Later children will have to read, that is, to decode the words of
people they may never have occasion to meet. In this process of
communication with increasingly anonymous individuals we see
a replication of something that recalls the history of languages
and of writing itself. The aim of this book is to trace this process in
children who have difficulty in learning to speak. By studying their
difficulties and possible ways of overcoming them we shall arrive
at some more general reflections on language itself.

The factors that cause children not to speak are extremely
varied. They cannot be reduced to psychological conflict. Nor
should we be content to seek an explanation in the neurological
side-effects of trauma or in cognitive failures. All these play some
part, but the surest way to bypass a real understanding is to seize
on a single kind of explanation to the exclusion of all others. In
therapeutic work, this can have grave consequences for those one
wishes to help. In scientific work, it may often lead to a degree
of intellectual dishonesty that consists in deliberately ignoring
important works because they depart from the line one wishes to
advocate. Unlike some other specialists, I shall advocate the need
for a composite explanation. I am convinced that, in spite of a
natural mental inclination to put forward a single type of causality
at the expense of all others, we must remain open to diversity,
which is not the same thing as confusion.

In my opinion, the obstacles to the acquisition of language are arranged in three main groups: the cognitive group, the aphasic group, and the symbolic group. The *cognitive group* concerns the automatic processes developed by the brain to perceive the world and our fellow beings in order, for example, to organize appropriate modes of behaviour in the area of vision and movement. The *aphasic group* refers to the totality of automatic processes that make it possible to proceed from thought to the sounds of speech and vice versa. Lastly, the *symbolic group*, which is the one most easily accessible to the psychoanalyst, takes account of everything in language that characterizes the relation between speakers and their own wishes, and their awareness of the thoughts of others.

Each one of these groups is coherent and partially independent, but none of them will alone afford a comprehensive understanding of the phenomena of language. They all exert a combined effect upon one another.

I shall attempt to examine the development of language by constantly emphasizing the dynamic exchange between these complementary groups. To do this I shall call on the three theoretical fields of psychoanalysis, linguistics, and cognitive development. The essential task will be to consider ways of combining the approaches of each of these disciplines.

As a rule I shall start from the material taken from one working session with a child. This will enable me to emphasize the individual features of that child's speech and the way in which these features become manifest, both of which contribute to the story of my work on that case.

During treatment, the majority of changes are imperceptible. It is only later that one realizes that there has been progress. In point of fact, it is only when we step back that we can observe the detail of a development or sequence of events, or explain certain paradoxes—why it is, for example, that a child can manage to pronounce a difficult word in one situation while having difficulty with a much simpler word in a different situation. This is what I shall try to explain.

It is true that the analysis of single case studies runs counter to some notions of what science is. In our time, science is understood to mean counting and large-scale statistics. Under the circumstances, however, this is not possible. Studies of the pathology of language development in children do not yet permit any serious use of statistics. Some works include graphs and curves, but the data often relate to fewer than twenty children.

Moreover, even when the population under study is sufficiently large, the problem remains. If statistics are to be of value they must be based upon a uniform coding of the data under consideration. Before any count is attempted, one must be sure that the same items have been classified under the same headings. We might decide to conduct a study of all the 'baas' and 'boos' pronounced by a child. But what would we then proceed to measure? Sounds, rather than words. If we want to make use of statistics, we must be sure to analyse reality without doing violence to its actual features. We may use statistics to understand better the anatomy of a roast chicken. But if the tools we use require that the raw material be minced, if we first have to transform our observable chicken into small, evenly diced pieces of white meat, I doubt if anyone could ever establish that the composition of the table-ready fowl includes, in a significant number of cases, two wings and two thighs. Where the language of children is concerned, quantitative studies impose so many restrictions that the subject is completely distorted, producing cubes of chicken instead of accepting the presence of wings and legs. The statistical approach in some ways guarantees scientific methodology. It was Aristotle who said, 'There is no knowledge other than general knowledge.' And recourse to statistics may be one guarantee—among others—of the general nature of this knowledge. But this is not the end of the quotation. The sentence goes on to deliver a stern warning: though there may be no knowledge other than general knowledge, 'only the particular exists'.

No one should expect to find in this book more than a few classifications or diagnoses. I am not opposed to these, but their use is a delicate matter. First, the evidence presented by children very frequently matches opposing clinical phenomena. Second, classifications sometimes prevent us from clearly observing the facts, and, above all, fix them in immutable form. The flexibility of a form of treatment, however, lies precisely in its mobility. We observe that in many contexts an insurmountable problem has a curious tendency to vanish in certain restricted circumstances, and we must be able to investigate the reasons for this. We must therefore avail ourselves of categories, not to pigeon-hole children, but, on the contrary, to pinpoint their individual symptoms and establish how each case differs from the clinical type which it otherwise fits. Furthermore, it is often by focusing on the difference that we enable the child to develop.

My purpose, then, is to listen to living language in the process of transformation and furnish the listening process with all the questions that can be raised by the diversity of contemporary thought, while paying attention to raw, humble, everyday facts rather than data garnered in a laboratory. In pursuing this aim I shall have recourse to varying modes of explanation, speaking by turns as psychoanalyst, linguist, and cognitive scientist. Once again, it seems to me vitally important to re-establish the links between what the social organization of knowledge, that is, the universities, divide, for reality demonstrates the need to combine these three approaches. Essentially, I shall try to tell stories, to understand them, and to relate what they can teach us, as I see it, about the nature of language.

1

What Game Are We Playing?

A Plea for a Measure of Diversity

I am a psychoanalyst, a linguist, and a writer. I realize that this is overdoing matters and my failure to make a choice is sometimes held against me. I tried for a long time to do so. Having failed, I tried to partition the different aspects of my linguistic activity, so as to present only one face at a time to each listener. Today, at the age of nearly 50, I have bowed to the obvious: it cannot be done. There would be about as much point in asking a frog to choose between water and terra firma. For all my unshakeable faith in the moral of the fairy tale, the frog in me has never been able to turn into a Prince Charming—or to choose one of the three modes of living in contact with language. I have therefore had to resign myself to the situation. Furthermore, I do not believe that this diversity of approaches is important. I love language in all its forms, and this is all that matters to me. This was why I started out as a diligent student of English grammar. It was why I began to write. And this is why I embarked on a long and gradual education which led me to become an analyst. And it is also the reason why I decided to specialize in work with children who could not speak. In one's first dealings with these children one feels something of the unease induced by primitive or unpolished art. The clumsiness of the beginner, but at the same time its power and violence. The children live immersed in an unforgiving fantasy-world. And the pleasure I derive in seeing them invent a story—their own story—probably encourages them to embroider it over the course of several weeks.

How does the process work in practice? I work in several centres where children who do not speak are referred to me. They are usually between 4 and 7 years old. I see them three times a week during the first year, twice a week in the second year, and once a week in the third. Sometimes the treatment lasts longer, especially when language difficulties are linked with psychological problems. The resolution of speech problems makes it possible to go further into the psychological ones.

It is my hope that my position and above all my purpose will by now be clear, and that it will be understood that I am not preaching any particular method. I prefer to suggest a way of looking at things in describing my way of working, which is to say, the way I am. Lastly, in writing this book, I have come to understand better some forms of behaviour in the children I have worked with, and this has been of practical benefit to me, while providing me with material for a number of insights into language.

Like a Drowsy Nanny

There is a fundamental difference between the nature of pedagogical work, aimed at teaching pupils to read or write, for example, and what I do with a child who does not speak or who speaks very badly. As a rule, the pedagogical assumption is that adults are the holders of knowledge which they wish to transmit to the child. They therefore, to some extent or other, expect the child to imitate the models they offer. At best, if they are at the cutting edge of their profession, the teachers endeavour to safeguard the child's creativity and do their best to make him 'discover' the knowledge that formerly they were happy to cram into him. In my view, there is no such thing as teaching, and cannot be. If they have worked out how to satisfy all their needs in five, six, or seven years of life, children who have not spoken are very much stronger than the most loquacious of teachers.

My general attitude is as unreflective as that of a teddy bear. Most of the time I operate by instinct and by playing, like a drowsy nanny. I let myself be guided, let my arm be twisted just as much as is necessary. It is only later, prompted by an urge to speculate and in order to meet my obligations as linguist, psychoanalyst, and academic, that I make the effort to consider what has happened, so as to deduce some guiding principles. Here I must be careful to ensure that these reflections do not distort the real picture of what actually occurs in the course of treatment.

I do my best, then, to be passive. This does not mean that I do nothing: I constantly let children lead me and I try to build on the basis of whatever they feel is needed to induce me to play. Letting them lead while I follow allows me to reverse the usual pedagogical direction. I suggest nothing that does not follow or respond to whatever they themselves suggest. If I do make a suggestion, instead of putting objects in their hands I place them between us and wait to see if they pick them up. Of course, whether or not they pick them up, and, if they do, the way in which they do so, are vital to an understanding of what takes place between us and to the subsequent choice of new suggestions.

On the whole I remain silent. I do not attempt to overwhelm the child with language or bring them into contact with texts, pictures, or songs. I establish a dialogue *without words*. This is because, before setting children on a path towards language, they must be given the feeling that they can be understood, even without words. This should be done without at the same time encouraging them to think that they can let me guess all their thoughts.

Essentially, then, I have no working method. But this does not mean that some recurrent features cannot be defined. In a way, these features are close to those which help an infant to develop speech with its mother. One of the founders of cognitive science, Jerome Bruner, realized that the way a mother plays with her child and aids its access to language follows certain fixed patterns, which he called 'formats' and which are quite the opposite of a method. There is something of this in my procedure. And yet it is different from the spontaneous action of a mother.

Most games played by a mother and child together develop with the mother facing her child. In my procedure this is not the case.

I sit beside the child and we look at the same thing. This seems insignificant, but it has several consequences: sitting side by side allows us to be directly aware of shared thoughts without needing to decode the signs that usually indicate what one is thinking. In contrast, if you are seated facing the child, on the other hand, you are obliged to point in order to draw attention to something. The child must therefore be able to interpret the motion of the finger as a pointing gesture, which is not self-evident. When you are seated beside a child at nightfall, and a car passes, for example, the movement of the headlights renders the object of thought visible: there is an immediate focusing of attention. The shared focus of thought no longer depends on the ability to interpret the gesture of pointing.

Piecing a Story Together

Language interests me only as a manifestation of psychological continuity, as a measure of the way relations are developed between individuals. Behind every word I feel the density of a dialogue continuing from one session to the next.

Unfortunately, all too often, before the actual history begins there is a prolonged period of prehistory, a somewhat ill-defined period in which I have difficulty thinking in terms of continuity, stories, or progress. This is particularly true of those children who are little inclined to communicate. There are those who play endless games that appear pointless, like lining up identical objects, toy fences, for example, then knocking them all down or overturning them one by one. All I can do is welcome the gesture, without attempting to present it as a well-defined scenario, and allow that this activity may have some point to it without seeking to discover what it is. If, then, in our first sessions children draw circles and fill them in with dots, I deduce that they have a notion of the difference between outside and inside, and that they are dramatizing a conception of space and marking its limits. In this light, their activity conveys some meaning. But I do not immediately think that the circle represents a face or a body, or that the dots are either two eyes, a nose, and a mouth (if one takes the circle to be the outline of a face), or babies (if one takes it as a body). But what is one to say to the child? Sometimes the act of saying 'a nose and a mouth' or 'babies' will give meaning to the activity. But at other times this kind of comment may spoil the pleasure and destroy the potential for meaning, as when one explains a witty remark to someone who has laughed without really knowing why.

In effect, in order to find the right wavelength, I allow the child to play with and manipulate me like a kitten with a ball of wool. I expect nothing in particular. I observe, I follow, I adjust to the rhythms of the child, and I say very little. Hence the effect of somnolence.

In Praise of Repetition

It is common, incidentally, for a child to begin by behaving like a kitten with a ball of wool: the same activity is repeated over and over again for hours. One little girl will spend several sessions marking dots on a blank sheet of paper. One boy will endlessly roll play-dough into little balls and arrange these in a miniature cupboard. Another will arrange blocks to form regular enclosures.

Yet another will push a toy car towards each of the people present. The nature of the repetition varies. A good repetition is one that consists of a *series of stages*.

Sometimes, during the first session, no repetition of this nature occurs. The child may, for example, spend the time simply rolling a marble under a glass. The action is repetitive but the total absence of variation, of phases or stages, means that there is no true repetition. There is only an activity as monotonous as the flow of a river. It is therefore necessary to introduce some discontinuity, some form of punctuation, to the extent that the child finds this acceptable: we may, for example, clap our hands each time the marble passes in front of us, as the important thing is to provide some pattern and divide the monotony into complementary segments. If there is to be repetition, there must be a return to an identical position, but the return must pass through a series of clearly differentiated stages.

For anyone who attends these first sessions, repetition—even when it augurs well—is extremely tedious. But the difficulty is much greater if the child does nothing at all, or becomes irritable and keeps changing from one activity to another without settling down. If children repeat just one activity, even if it is only the ritualized and monotonous rolling of the marble under the glass, the first point has already been won. If the repetition comprises several stages, or if children permit outside intervention—if they react when we mark dots beside their dots on a sheet of paper, or take balls of play-dough offered to them and put them in the cupboard with their own—we have every reason to be more than satisfied.

The fact that the child says nothing should not disturb us. I say little as long as the child does not wish to speak. In the early stages I may not say a single word. The aim at this stage is to establish a stable pattern of repetition and to show that this interests me. Later it will be possible to do other things. Children who push the toy car will start to indicate, before setting it in motion, to whom they intend to send it. They may allow us to complicate the game by repeatedly sticking a piece of play-dough onto the roof of the car and detaching it when the car reaches the end of its run. After a number of sessions a routine will be established. First they dispatch the car without any play-dough, then they leave the play-dough on the car, and finally they remove the play-dough when the car arrives. In this way a ritual composed of a series of stages is established, and each event becomes predictable. That is, as we shall see, each event becomes *meaningful*.

A Prelude to the Sign

It is essential that a pattern of stable and differentiated repetition be established. This is a prerequisite to speech because it opens the door to the world of signs. In a series of phases, each event effectively becomes the premonitory sign of the next. At the same time, it is a copy of the preceding one. If the pattern of repetition described above is established, the movement of the toy car with the play-dough on its roof intact at the end of its run signals to the child and to me the arrival of the next stage, when the play-dough will be removed. Each stage serves as a sign of the stage that will follow. Of course, its status as a premonitory sign is based on the memory of previous sessions and on the knowledge that we both share. But in our eyes, the toy car's journey with its play-dough assumes a particular value. It is no longer merely an event in a series of events. It is the signal of a forthcoming event and the reminder of a past event. By virtue of the established pattern, each stage becomes a *signifier* representing two things at once, the preceding and following stages. We have here the creation of a sign, since a visible signifier, a gesture, is linked with an invisible signified.

In the confined universe we have constructed, communication has become possible. It has a framework. It is usually at this point that I permit myself to say a word or two to punctuate what is happening. But the greatest difficulty is in actually building the framework. When one meets somebody for the first time, the problem is not so much one of communicating one's news as of framing the exchange, being sure that they 'see clearly' the topic of the conversation. The fundamental problem of all communication lies in defining the common ground, in all senses of this term. And repetition is an easy way of doing this. In the infinity of everything that can be said or thought, it makes it possible to isolate a fragment. Here the fragment is a very simple one, containing no more than a few objects and gestures. The thoughts to be communicated can be easily grasped. Even a child who remains silent can be sure that I understand.

Slight Disturbances

At a certain point in the treatment, the pattern of repetition becomes established. Sessions assume an unchanging order, with the same words occurring at set moments. It becomes tedious. It is then up to me to vary the session so as to deliberately stall it.

Experience shows that children make no effort to conceptualize a process unless confronted with a divergence between their expectations and what actually happens. As long as a repetitive sequence unfolds smoothly, they make no attempt to conceptualize. But when the session takes an unexpected turn the child attempts to understand why. There is no conceptualization until some kind of obstruction appears. Drivers usually reach for the gear lever without forming a mental picture of its position relative to the steering wheel. If asked whether the gear lever is mounted on the floor, the dashboard or the steering column, they will need to go through the motion of changing gear before replying, as this automatic activity is unaccompanied by any conceptualization. If, on the other hand, the gearbox is faulty and they have to nurse the lever into gear, they will immediately be able to say where the lever is, since the mental image (in the crude sense) comes to mind when the sequence is disrupted. It is as if the blocking of the reflex response were a necessary precondition to its explicit formulation. By disrupting the child's spontaneous scenario I seek to promote some limited conceptualization.

Once the ritual is established I try to disrupt it to create an unforeseen situation that will lead children to imagine the situation they wish to return to, assuming they want to re-establish the routine. Before taking action, they must first be aware of the difference between their expectations and reality. Most commonly the disruption hinges on the absence of something. It consists in removing some object to a hiding place close enough for it to be recovered. For example, I may put the play-dough that the children usually play with on a shelf other than the one where it is normally kept, but still within reach. They will then need to conceptualize what they want, realize that it differs from what they see, and, if they want to, convey to me what they intend to do to minimize the deviation.

If ill-timed, these disruptions do not have the desired effect. Children will respond by showing either agitation or a lack of interest. For example, if when I move the play-dough they begin running about, or are downcast and do not even try to find what is missing, this means they cannot yet tolerate the slightest deviation. If the response is crude and unfruitful, I shall have missed my goal, but at least my attempt has been acknowledged.

I recall a child whose game consisted of rolling a toy car towards me. One day I trapped it under the lid of a box. I kept it hidden in this way, expecting him to point to the lid in order to indicate that I should let the car out. Instead, he lunged at the lid and raised it by force to reclaim his car. I repeated the exercise several times in the hope that he would decide to point at the lid instead. But each time he lunged to lift the lid, take back the car and push it along again. My ploy was to no avail. The child could not point to the hidden car or the obstacle. How should his response be assessed? He tolerates the disruption, it is true, since he does not begin running about in all directions and he continues the game by once again pushing the car towards me. But this disruption is not fruitful as he is content to overcome it by force. There is no development, no enrichment. My action produces no variation. Seeing that this does not work, I try something else. I take a sheet of paper, fold it to form a tunnel and put it on the table. Then I show the child how to push the car through the tunnel so that it emerges at the other end. This time the idea is accepted and the game works. Having been on the other side of the table, he now comes round to my side and spontaneously pushes the car through the tunnel.

Tolerance of variation, then, has its limits. Some inventions may be integrated into the game, while others may not. Sometimes we can understand why a child is intolerant of variation. In our example, we may conclude that the child cannot bear the thought that the car is kept hidden for a long time. He is not altogether sure that it still exists when he cannot see it. He must therefore lift the lid immediately in order to see it again, reclaim it, and play with it. In order to point to the lid he would need to be sure of its permanent existence. To be sure, he knows that things continue to exist when absent, since he looks for the car. But he is not sure if things remain as he has seen them, since he does not point in the direction of the thing he cannot see. In the case of the tunnel, on the other hand, the disappearance of the toy car is temporary. Now he can admit my disruption. It amuses him. The visible–invisible–visible sequence becomes acceptable.

Conflict Incited by Adult Discourse

The mere act of verbalizing the actions of children, even if this elicits no verbal response from them, often produces a variation in their original pattern. This variation is in fact their response to a disruption induced by the words of the adult, for to describe to children what they are doing is often to put into words a conflict that their game tends to push into the background.

Here, for example, is a sequence from a session with a little girl whose story I will tell later. Kim takes a number of fences and forms them into two adjoining enclosures. This is a game she has frequently played. She then signals that I should hand her various animals, which she proceeds to sort: in one pen she puts all the animals whose mouths are closed, and in the other all those whose mouths are open.

'Oh yes, this pen is for the ones that bite and that one is for the ones that don't bite,' I say, wishing to draw her attention to this. At once she asks me for the big crocodile, which often stands for the mother in our games. On the face of it, this is the animal most inclined to bite. But this crocodile poses a problem because it has a hinged jaw that allows its mouth to be either open or closed. Holding it in her hand, she hesitates, uncertain where to put it. She tries to put it in the non-biters' pen, but says, 'It can't go in there.' Finally, unable to choose, she decides to place it outside both pens on its back, belly up. This animal which can either bite or not bite assumes the position of a dead animal.

This action is then repeated: one by one she takes the animals from both enclosures and turns them on their backs, as if a plague had struck. Faced with this scene of extreme violence I feel somewhat uncomfortable. Seeking reassurance, I enquire whether the animals are actually dead or merely asleep. She at once looks for and finds in the biters' enclosure a little crocodile that lacks a hinged jaw and, as a result of rough handling by other children, has lost the top of its head. It has only a blood-red lower jaw. With this maimed animal she rubs the belly of the big crocodile, which she has placed outside the pens, giving it, as she says, a kiss. Having received this life-restoring 'kiss', the big crocodile can stand on its feet again, as can all the other animals.

Here I have intervened on two occasions: the first time to make clear to Kim the basis of her sorting operation and indicate that

I understand her wish to remove danger. My speaking leads her to attempt partially to negate the point I have made by asking me for the big crocodile. Because of its hinged jaw, this crocodile belongs in neither group, or can have a place in either, or can be somewhere else entirely. She opts for the latter, placing the big crocodile on the outside. But in speaking to Kim of an animal *qui mord* (which bites) I must have provoked the memory of a similar word with quite different meaning, *mort* (dead). At least, this is how I understand her gesture of turning the animal onto its back. Yet, when it is in this position we cannot tell if it is dead or asleep. Hence my discomfiture and my second interruption to have Kim make another distinction. Here, although there is nothing that might allow me to state this with certainty, I feel that the little girl shares my unease and responds by bringing in the little crocodile with the broken jaw to caress the belly of the bigger one. The baby has features of the two groups to which it is related. As a crocodile he is a biter. But having a broken jaw he is one of the 'bitten'. He is therefore enlisted to take care of his exhausted mother.

Outwardly my first remark about separating the biters from the non-biters was simply a way of putting into words what Kim was doing. But it was also a way of verbally re-establishing a link between the biters and non-biters, whereas Kim's game consisted in preventing contact between the two groups. My words restored the conflict. Contrary to what took place with the child whose toy car I concealed, this was not a case of prompting conceptualization by producing an absence, but of expressing in words the conflict played out in the game. By saying that the biting animals were separated from those that did not bite I was endorsing the division expressed by gesture. But I was also verbally constructing a connection between the two groups and awakening the fear of conflict which had led to the separation. It was this fear that had caused Kim to act out this scenario. My second intervention was again designed to establish and then express the elements of a conflict. I felt a slight unease on seeing the big mother crocodile lying on her back because this position seemed to suggest death, sleep, or something else. But it was my spoken words that brought out the contrast by explicitly differentiating death and sleep.

Similar, Dissimilar

We have seen how a child constructs variations within the stable patterns of a session. These variations are a first step towards applying the notion of what is the same and what is different. But there is another way, one of breaking free from the dimension of time. We shall see later how Rachid spent several of our sessions finding similarities and differences, not to vary the scenarios but to discover how similar but not identical objects differed when handled. Rachid likes doors. They facilitate games of hide-and-seek, and allow one to pass through. Their sameness of function appeals to him. But since a swing door, a sliding door, and an ordinary door do not entail quite the same motions, Rachid seizes on the differences between them. Here he is faced with a double movement. On the one hand, he has a tendency to confuse all doors that are suitable for hide-and-seek. On the other, he grasps the difference between each type of door that requires a particular motion to open or close it. This means that his conceptualization of the thing known as 'a door' contains a conflict. In one sense a door 'is like' any other door in that it allows things to disappear and reappear. But each door also differs from other doors because it slides, swings to and fro, or can be opened with a key. Thus, in an object that in itself is of no interest, Rachid discovers the consistency and contrasts that are necessary for all constructs of the mind. A door, like any other object, is built at the meeting-point of two properties: one that it shares with all others, the other that is its own.

As soon as a single object is defined by two corresponding gestures, it has two properties and so acquires 'density'. This is not simply by virtue of having two properties; it is also because, by virtue of each of these properties, it enters into a specific comparative relationship with other elements which are not featured in the context. Let us imagine Rachid playing with a swing door: the fact that it enables one to play hide-and-seek establishes a direct congruence with both a sliding door and an ordinary door; but the fact that it is activated by a forward motion, and has a degree of resistance, forms a contrast with the sliding door (which opens laterally) and the ordinary door (which opens and closes in one simple movement). The density results from the existence of two properties, each of which forms an antagonistic connection with a constant category of absent objects.

The elements being compared, in this case doors, thus come to constitute alternatives. Whatever their type, they all facilitate games in which things can appear and disappear. They are all well suited to the game of hide-and-seek. But the choice of one type precludes recourse to another. If I decide to make my teddy bear disappear behind the sliding door of a low cabinet, I am declining to use the swing door of the cupboard.

The moment a slot may be filled by different elements of the same type, while choosing one means rejecting the others, a paradigm is constituted. This is a kind of relationship found in language at all levels.

Playing with objects of the same type is also of interest in that it suggests links with the outside world. For example, when Rachid plays with a sliding door in front of me, he calls to mind the Metro and all that can happen in it. The swing doors remind him of his life in the corridors of his school. And when I open the 'normal' door of my office—a single door that locks with a key—and invite him in, some part of his own home finds its way into our session. Each of these doors is the point of departure for a game that unfolds before me but recalls a different context, another universe—school, home, or the Metro.

Repetition and change, presence and absence, continuity and comparison, conjunction and disjunction are, as we shall see, terms that can serve to characterize some of the crystallizing moments that occur in the course of work with a child who does not speak.

2

Fabien:
Thinking without Words

'I have forgotten the word I wanted to say, and my disembodied thought is returning to the kingdom of shadows,' wrote the Russian poet, Osip Mandelstam, who was none the less pleased at finding other words to express his lapse of memory and his anxiety.

When words elude a child, what can that child do to feel at ease with its thoughts, to build on what it perceives, what it sees, what it knows, without fear of letting its thoughts 'return to the kingdom of shadows'? And if words keep letting children down, how can they be made to understand that, in spite of everything, it would be a pity if they were to reject such a splendid instrument?

What follows is my account of three years' work with a child, work that enabled me to understand how the function of symbol-forming develops when the linguistic mechanism is lacking.

First Meeting with Fabien

Physically, Fabien was a good-looking lad with brown hair and an open, lively face. He was a little shy at first, chiefly because of the embarrassment caused by his difficulty in expressing himself. When I first saw him he was nearly 7 and could manage only a few words, never more than a monosyllable at a time.

During our first two sessions, Fabien drew. He drew two wolves with babies inside them. Then he took our box of toys, upturned it, stood two plastic tigers on it as if on the plinth of a statue and made them growl. Turning to me, he pointed to them and said 'morts', in such a way that it was impossible to tell whether he meant *ils sont morts* (they are dead) or *ils mordent* (they bite). During a subsequent session he made them move a little and then said *non morts* (not dead). My part in his game was to introduce other animals to the tigers, who regularly ate them. The animals that were 'not dead' endlessly consumed the others, who died. As is so often the case, the confusion between animals that bit and those which were dead was not merely a result of linguistic confusion; it appeared to be connected to thought processes that were unwilling to distinguish the two.

In the early stages, there were many sessions in which everything hinged on appearance, disappearance, and separation. Sometimes Fabien hid in a little low cabinet which he could crawl into only with great difficulty. He would hide, wait a moment, then kick the door open and slowly climb out. Watching him made me think of the process of birth and I pictured him struggling to emerge from his mother's body. This continued until the day when Fabien acted out a birth scene, this time in the role of director. From the toy-box he selected the felt cut-out figures of a mother and child. He proceeded to coat them with red chalk and play the scene with gripping realism. He seemed to have cast himself as doctor. Since we were in an office that contained a sink with running water, he washed the mother and child. At the end of the session, being a little anxious about what he had acted out in front of me without my intervening, he went to the waiting-room to convey to his father what had happened.

Despite the absence of language, Fabien had fantasies that are common in children of his age. The baby wolves from our first session returned with great regularity, constantly transformed into new guises. As there was no verbal interaction, my role consisted in observing what Fabien could enact without language, and in putting him at ease with the feeling that he could have an exchange with me by means of fairly precise play-acting, without this necessarily being verbalized.

Gradually language came into place. Even if the process was a little slow for my liking, his vocabulary developed. Syntax, however, remained non-existent. It did not appear until much later, when one day, indignant at some prohibition of mine, he declared that I was a *crotte de nez* (a bit of snot). Rarely has an insult given me such satisfaction! But why should this have emerged in a moment of anger? How could anger make it possible to establish an explicit grammatical link ('of') between two words? Could it be a delayed repetition of a ritual expression Fabien had picked up from his schoolfriends? This explanation can be discounted, as he must also have heard people say 'le livre de Paul', not 'livre Paul', yet in phrases of this type he did not build in the preposition. Fabien's feelings towards me must have found a kind of outlet in this insult, and the release of tension suddenly made it possible for him to construct a link between the two words. It was as if the tension had helped him to overcome his linguistic blockages and this tension enabled him to connect the two words in one phrase. It might also be suggested that for Fabien 'bit of snot' was a single word of three syllables. If so, even that would have marked substantial progress compared to his utterances at the beginning. 'Bit of snot' is much longer than a monosyllable such as 'dead' (*mort*) and more firmly connected than the two coupled monosyllables 'not dead' (*non morts*). But I believe that, even if 'of' was not fully separable from the nouns, the expression as a whole did not form a unit, simply because Fabien used both nouns independently and understood their meaning. The expression 'bit of snot' clearly entailed a grammatical connection between two independent words.

This episode, all the more curious because it did not actually mark the beginning of Fabien's use of syntax, recalls research into different circuits of language in the study of aphasia. I remember a man who suffered from chronic Broca's aphasia and was incapable of articulating anything, yet when driving his car he had no difficulty in letting fly with 'These women drivers!' on seeing a woman driving badly. The circuit of his 'automatic language'—to use the phrase applied by Jackson, the famous neurologist was perfectly preserved. As we shall see later in the case of Kim an impaired linguistic apparatus can more easily be mobilized in highly charged situations than in those in which neutral, conscious, considered speech is appropriate.

A few months later, overcoming his anxiety at separation, Fabien agreed to join a group excursion to the snowfields, without having anybody to act as his interpreter. On his return, his speech had made clear progress. Fabien seemed to want to understand what was happening to him. At the end of one session, his mother came to meet us in the waiting-room and told me that Fabien had recently wanted to know whether his delayed language development was 'from birth', like the mark on the neck of one of his friends. I replied—in Fabien's presence—that, even when speech difficulties are present from birth, things could change, and this was now happening.

Strangely, the moment Fabien began to speak better, his games became the poorer. They shed their violence, but with it they lost their symbolic richness. During our sessions his rituals became rather wearisome, consisting of playing marbles and endless games of football between two chairs in the office. Furthermore, any word I happened to utter, anything that went beyond the strict requirements of the game or ever so slightly resembled a commentary —let alone an interpretation —provoked him to anger. He called me to order, exclaiming 'Don't tell your life story!' It was also impossible to play cards, dominoes, or draughts: when he was in danger of losing, Fabien began to cheat. He had no more time for the rules of a game than for those of syntax.

Vaguely seeking a way to make him conscious of the need to observe rules, and therefore giving in to the temptation to teach, I one day brought with me the equipment needed for a very simple conjuring trick, the eggcup trick. An eggcup with a lid is opened before the spectator, who sees a red ball inside. The conjurer takes out the ball and puts it in his pocket, then closes the lid of the eggcup. He asks the spectator to blow, lifts the lid, and the ball has mysteriously returned. Having witnessed this act as a spectator, Fabien wanted to reproduce the illusion. I explained it to him. In his impatience he missed out some steps, aware, however, that if he did not follow the steps in sequence, if he did not comply with my instructions, the trick would not work. The rules of the trick cannot be disregarded without ruining the effect, giving the game away, and falling back into the realm of ordinary logic. He was thus obliged to obey a rule in order to 'cheat'.

With time we progressed to games requiring a partner. He was content—or almost content—to play draughts, even when he lost. And gradually his syntax, in writing at least, developed and diversified, although his oral expression remained fragmented. I often found myself between two stools: anxious not to hurry events, so as to give him time to absorb the language he was acquiring (nothing would have grieved me more than to hear him speak in the painfully strict diction of the ill-trained aphasia sufferer), and worried by the passage of time. Shortly before Easter his family came to see me. Fabien was tired and had no liking for school. In short, he was depressed. From a conversation with his mother I learned that Fabien's little brother, four years younger than he, was beginning to speak and that, to make things worse, the dentist had just forbidden Fabien to suck his thumb before going to sleep as this would make his teeth crooked. Thus he was being displaced from the position of youngest child, while the younger brother could do as he pleased.

Fabien Coping

After the holidays, Fabien came to a session carrying a stretchy elastic thread with a little soft hand at the end of it and showed me how to throw it at a wall. 'It sticks,' he said. And he proceeded to arrange a contest to see which of us was best at making this hand stick. After a while, he explained with some difficulty that this toy did not belong to him. A boy he had met in the waiting-room had lent it to him. Thereupon, as he tried to stretch the elastic attached to the hand, it broke. Fabien was anxious. The hand actually belonged to the boy's brother. Fabien would not dare admit to him that he had broken it. There was only one solution: he had heard that the toy came from a nearby bakery. We therefore had to go there together. After letting him insist at some length, I finally agreed to go. In the waiting-room we encountered his father, and Fabien took the opportunity to ask him for some money. Downstairs, outside the bakery, he was too shy to go in. At last he plucked up his courage and darted in: 'Any sticky hands?' The woman replied that she had none left. Fortunately, on leaving we chanced upon some in a nearby toy shop. Fabien was delighted and bought one for himself and another for his friend. Back in my office, his attitude changed. He lined up the chairs one behind the other, inviting me to take the back seat while he took the front one. We were in an aeroplane. He was the pilot. We took off. For the first time in a long while Fabien interrupted his ritual without reverting to his earlier violence with the wolves, biting animals, and birth pangs.

His linguistic progress continued, but a year had passed. Fabien was growing. Often he preferred to say as little as possible or nothing at all rather than risk a faulty utterance. Anger became his preferred means of expression. Even so, I was reassured by his need for contact, the speed with which he made friends, his physical adroitness, and the pleasure we both derived from our sessions.

About two years after the start of his treatment, during a session which promised to be no different from the others, he at last produced utterances that seemed to me to indicate definitively that he had gained access to structured language.

On this occasion he entered my office carrying a tennis ball and asked me to hold a cushion against the wall for him to aim at. A little later he changed targets and threw the ball at the box of toys, scattering the figures all over the floor. I arranged them in a rough circle. He then suggested a game to test my powers of observation: I had to take a careful look at the disposition of figures, then look away so that he could rearrange them, then look back at them to spot the differences. I complied. When he finally let me turn round, I studied the arrangement thoroughly, but in vain—I could not see what changes he had made. Seeing my puzzlement, he said with some pride: 'Ça m'étonne tu trouves' (lit. it surprises me you find). This undoubtedly meant, 'Ça m'étonnerait que tu trouves' (I'd be surprised if you found any).

We continued our game for a moment, then he changed his mind and returned to the cushions. He took a cushion, threw it up in the air and punched it, saying: 'Take that, Monsieur Boileau!' After this he mimed a karate bout by himself. On television there was a Japanese serial in which the hero is an invincible 8-year-old karate fighter; I asked him if he had seen it. He replied immediately: 'Mort, le maître!' (lit. dead, the master). The fact was that in the serial the boy is under the constant guidance of his long-dead ancestor, whom he summons up by praying at critical moments. I also remembered that one year Fabien had been much impressed by a schoolteacher who had told him that he was suffering from an incurable disease. And, of course, I also felt myself the target of this foreshadowing of death, especially as a short while ago his game had entailed throwing punches at me. I said nothing. Fabien abandoned his karate bout. Out of breath, he sat down, then got up again, picked up the cushion and punched it again, this time saying, 'Ton fils, il est mort' (lit. your son, he is dead).

'Ça m'étonne tu trouves,' like 'Ton fils, il est mort,' was a statement of infinitely greater complexity than any that Fabien had formulated up to now, a complexity that was not a matter of length but of structure. For different reasons, these sentences demonstrate some ability to construct an utterance while changing, in the process, the function and the value of the parts.

An utterance usually comprises two essential parts. The first serves to attract attention to what is to be said. It defines the limits of the conversation, the subject to be addressed. This is the 'theme'. The second part expresses what the speaker actually wishes to convey, the 'rheme'. If I say, 'Yesterday the teacher gave us a dictation,' the term 'teacher' is not simply a way of introducing a character, but of inviting listeners to turn their minds to the world of school and preparing them to take in what follows. The second part, 'gave us a dictation', effectively expresses what it was that motivated the utterance.

The paradox is that in the sequence of discourse the expression of the theme precedes the actual message, the rheme, while in the mental progression leading to the definitive utterance it is the other way round. It is the most important point, the rheme, that comes to mind first, followed by the words that prepare the hearer to receive it. The sequence in speech is the reverse of the sequence of the emergence of thoughts. Some memory is required, a retentive capacity, in order to keep in mind what one wishes to say while formulating the introduction, and to disclose it only after that introduction. One must also be able to alter the function of the constituent parts. This entails great flexibility in the speech apparatus. It is this flexibility that Fabien lacks. As a result he says, for example, 'Dead, the master' rather than 'The master dead.' The thing that is important for him to say, the thing that causes him to speak, the rheme—the fact of death—comes before the thing that enables his hearer to understand of whom he is speaking. When Fabien says 'dead', it can only refer to 'the master'. Only after this does he clarify for my benefit what is obvious to him.

In everyday speech, of course, the theme does not always precede the rheme. A statement such as 'She gave us a dictation, yesterday, the teacher' is fully acceptable, and displays the sequence 'rheme, theme'. The choice really depends on what has already been said during the conversation. There are times when the theme cannot be chosen as the starting point. When we wish to rebut a point on which our interlocutor seeks to extract agreement, that is, when we wish to differ, we must begin by asserting our own viewpoint—the rheme—and then indicate the point at issue to which this refers. The statement 'I'd be surprised if you found any', for example, is preferred to 'If you found any, I'd be surprised'. We begin with our main point, 'I'd be surprised', which expresses doubt, before signalling what this applies to in a subordinate clause. In the absence of common ground, of a consensus that might serve as our initial theme, we take as our base the expression of our disagreement. The rheme is thus placed first. This is what may explain Fabien's sentence 'Ça m'étonne tu trouves' (It surprises me you find), which in this case follows the expected order, though the syntax is faulty and the link between the two elements is marked only by intonation, the 'que' having been dropped.

For all its imperfections, a sentence like this indicates considerable progress. It articulates elements whose value changes when they are brought together. Each part of the sentence forms a coherent whole on its own. 'It surprises me', on the one hand, and 'tu trouves' on the other, could be two independent assertions. But the rising intonation of the first part indicates lack of completion, the fact that this segment depends on the segment that follows. Although it is an autonomous assertion, it begs to be completed. Each of the two parts is at once autonomous and linked. The final sentence represents the assembly of these two opposing statements.

In the case of 'Your son, he is dead,' the progress is even more marked. This time Fabien observed the 'theme, rheme' order. He placed 'he is dead' in second position, although this was the first thing to come to mind. How did he manage this? We may venture at least one hypothesis. Fabien had already introduced the subject of death in 'dead, the master'. If we take the statement on its own, disregarding the dialogue as a whole, the theme is clearly 'ton fils', and the rheme 'il est mort'. But in the broader context of our conversation, the idea of death constituted the framework, the shared theme, the unifying notion. Here, by contrast, it is the identity of the deceased (my son) that causes Fabien to speak in order to define a new rheme. The element that is the theme at one level becomes the rheme at another.

It is, no doubt, this variability that Fabien is exploiting. He does not have to hold back a rheme while placing the theme first, since 'your son' is actually his 'true' rheme. He needs to pinpoint a new victim in order to erase in some way the previous victim. For, in multiplying the number of deaths, he confuses the issue and thus reduces the force of his feelings of aggression against me. It is as if Fabien were saying, 'On second thoughts, it wasn't the teacher who died. It was somebody else. I made a mistake.' The victim's changed identity thus constitutes the true rheme. Hence its position in the sentence. Moreover, the confusion is with the associations also present concerning the victim. In naming 'your son' as the deceased, Fabien is merely choosing a relative of mine. I remain the target, even if this time I am targeted not through the figure of 'a master' but through a boy of his own age. Language thus permits Fabien to assemble a linguistic structure in which the same element can be linked with contradictory values while remaining coherent. This is the essential point.

Words, Syllables, Meaning

From this session on I felt reassured, even if the progress had not been linear and even if Fabien's linguistic development was as yet insufficient to provide an alternative to provocative behaviour. For despite more fluent syntax—by this I mean the use of the imperfect in locutions such as 'No, I was saying that you could stop', or the use of pronouns—if mislaid objects were mentioned in our conversations, for example, Fabien would spit in my office. It was as though, at such moments, owing to his difficulties, language became an additional source of tension rather than a calming influence. Later, as he developed the ability to write, the agitation caused by language became more manageable. The fact of being able to preserve words on paper, without being tormented by the fear of having them elude him, must have done something to reduce Fabien's anxiety in relation to everything that involves language. Writing also helped to foster in him an awareness of the mechanical dimension of language and of the way in which this aspect of language caused difficulty for him.

He came to appreciate the problems posed by the syllabic structure of words, for example. To make him practise breaking down words into syllables without hurting his feelings, I modified a game that he invented. Being physically quite adroit, Fabien was particularly fond of a rather special kind of throwing contest: the object of the game was to throw our coloured pencils into the waste-paper basket. To find the range I had quickly developed a habit of swinging the pencil towards the target, while uttering a short sentence chopped into syllables: 'At-ten-tion I am go-ing to throw', as if the rhythm of the syllables were a way of judging the trajectory and a magic formula in the style of 'abracadabra' (and equally effective). Very soon I heard Fabien repeating my short, rhythmic sentence under his breath as he looked on, watching for the moment when I would release the pencil. Soon he began using the expression when taking aim himself. As I progressively varied my statements, Fabien began to use longer and more varied sentences, in rhythmic speech. In this way he came to produce utterances correctly without being constrained to use the automatic circuit that had enabled him to produce 'bit of snot'.

Networks of Signifiers

Wishing to exploit Fabien's interest in the written word, I decided to introduce a computer. At an early stage, Fabien dictated words to me from an illustrated dictionary, while I typed them on the screen. I then proposed that he should dictate whole sentences to me. Finally we swapped roles. I dictated to him the statement, 'Mummy has bought a strawberry tart.' As soon as he had typed it I showed him how the computer makes it easy to delete words in order to change them. He could, for instance, replace 'tart' with something else. Nothing occurred to him, so I said, 'What about the thing you lick, like this?' and proceeded to mime the action of holding a cornet and licking an ice-cream. I expected him to respond with the word *glace* (ice-cream), but instead he replied, *sucette* (lollipop). Although somewhat surprised, I inserted the word in place of 'tart'.

I then noticed a curious phenomenon: when he reread the text aloud, on pronouncing the word *sucette* his face brightened, as if he had only just grasped the meaning of the word. Since he was dictating the word to me, he was plainly aware of it. And yet it seemed as if it was only now that the word attached itself to something more than the word *sucer* (to suck), thanks to the context provided by the sentence. As if until now the word *sucette* had been no more than a simple derivative of the verb *sucer*, without conjuring up any particular object in his mind. It was as if the written form had set him on the track of its meaning. As if it was necessary to have the word written in a sentence in order to register the fact that this derivative of the verb could also serve to designate an object in the real world.

It was at about this time that Fabien began to take pleasure in toying with the systematic workings of language, of the shape and structure of words. His interests included the morphology of verbs, which change their endings according to tense and person but preserve the same root, and that of derivatives, which make it possible to form connections between words, such as 'fish', 'fishmonger', 'fishmonger's shop'.

Access to Poetry

Writing was thus crucial in enabling Fabien to grasp certain aspects of language that his difficulties with speech prevented him from appreciating. No doubt things would have remained at this level had it not been for the discovery of metaphor.

One evening our conversation turned to sharks. He asked if I had a book about them. I stalled for a moment and tried to hedge, asking him to draw one, then offering to draw one myself, but to no avail. He insisted, so I relented,

In the library we found a lavishly illustrated book that showed all kinds of sharks: hammerhead sharks, grey nurse sharks, tiger sharks. Fabien looked at the pictures while I read out the names to him one by one. Suddenly he stopped in surprise. He had just realized that the shark known as the grey nurse was not a nurse, that the one called the tiger shark was not a tiger, and the one called the hammerhead shark had a solid square head but not a hammer. Two words for the same picture. This was the birth of 'as if', demonstrating the metaphoric shift from word to object.

This moment was apparently the fundamental experience that enabled Fabien to diversify his conception of the function of a word, showing him that one and the same word can sometimes *denote* and sometimes *describe*.

I do not claim that it was a sudden opening of the floodgates. Nor do I claim that he previously thought that a word was inseparable from an object or that this experience represented a watershed, but I do believe that something happened that evening in his conception of the relation between language and the world. Among the prime catalysts was the fact that having been able to take in at one glance a photograph and two words denoting a single animal counted for much. No doubt Fabien's linguistic difficulties prevented him from having two aural signifiers and the representation of an imaginary referent coexist in his field of thought.

Thanks to the book, the connection between the three elements had been established. Fabien was now able to use one word in two different ways: as a means of reference, such as 'shark' in 'tiger shark', and as metaphors, such as 'hammerhead', 'grey nurse', or 'tiger' coupled with the signifier 'shark'. Two words for the same thing: this is our starting point. When a single object may be designated by two different words, the word and the object can no longer be confused. But when the names of objects escape us permanently, how are we to link an object to its name? The experience of metaphor enabled Fabien to grasp the essence of the symbolic function of language. It is the expression of an outlook upon the real world, giving it coherence without being a fragment that might be confused with it. If we say of an irregular shape, 'It isn't square', we are marking it off and giving it meaning. But this does not add anything to the referent itself. In addition, a fairly fluent sense of language is required to make observations of this nature, for in situations of this kind words serve less to communicate meaning than to clarify perception and to classify.

A Language with which to Classify

One day Fabien brought with him an educational toy consisting of pictures of objects that have several characteristics: a large red square, a small green square, a small red circle, a large green rectangle, etc. The game consists in arranging them in a particular way. They have to be placed on a diagram of a tree. Each 'leaf' at the end of a branch defines the position of one picture and one only. The choice of 'the right place' relies on successive sorting. If, for example, we pick up the picture of the big green triangle, we go to the space at the foot of the tree. Two branches rise from this space, a red branch (on which there is a red window) and a green one (with a green window). We follow along the green branch, which leads to a new fork where the branch divides into one for triangles (a window on it displays a triangle) and one for circles (with a window displaying a circle). Once we have chosen the 'triangle' branch, it leads to a last fork where we must choose between a big branch and a small branch. At the end of this branch, where the leaf is shown, we can at last place our picture.

The game compels one to establish a hierarchy according to the characteristics of the objects depicted and to proceed sequentially through them all.

Among the indices that serve to classify the objects, there is one that is particularly difficult as it represents negative options. There is one branch, for example, with a square barred by a cross, and another with a red patch similarly barred. These correspond respectively to the options 'non-square' and 'non-red'. This kind of classification calls for the deployment of verbalization. Direct comparison between the picture on the branch and the one we are seeking to place is unavailing. Visual similarities no longer help. We cannot identify a barred square, representing non-square, with a round picture. We must proceed using the medium of language.

When Fabien tackled the sorting process he was therefore confronted with a need to verbalize. Owing to his difficulties, language was an irksome thing to be used as little as possible, only when there was no other way of making oneself understood. Here he had no reason to resort to words. For a long time Fabien pondered the barred square. While he was considering this, I murmured, as if to myself, 'That must mean "not square" [*pas carré*]'. He understood at once, which did not surprise me. But, more importantly, he seized on the tool offered by the word itself and repeated in a whisper 'not square' for the barred square, then 'not green' and 'not a triangle' for the other slots. In this way he solved the problem. Fabien thus came to understand the importance of language, not just in order to be understood by others (which had long been painful for him), but to engage in dialogue with oneself. Negation, like metaphor, is an operation with its roots in the innermost depths of the symbolic function of language. We can see here how this function is intertwined with the mechanical dimension of language.

Portrait of the Therapist as a Word-Swallower

I now come to the way we subsequently extended our work of reading and comprehension. Fabien was in the habit of bringing with him books of stories of about fifty pages, with repeated episodes that he remembered with difficulty from one session to the next. One day he brought a different kind of story, about a demon called Filologue, who steals articles and prepositions from a boy in return for doing his homework for him. The similarity with our own respective positions was striking. The boy in the story was developing an ungrammatical language, not so distant from that of Fabien, while my linguistic assistance lent me the role of a potential Filologue. The first time he brought me the book, Fabien asked me to read it to him. He listened with great interest, trying as he did so to put back the missing articles and prepositions in the boy's sentences. I never explicitly emphasized the parallel with ourselves. Yet, following this fictionalization of his difficulties, Fabien himself took charge of his reading activities and gradually established a certain distance between himself and me. This distance permitted him to accept that I was not simply the person who helped him to develop speech.

His discovery of me as someone with a life outside our sessions occurred quite fortuitously, as is often the case. One evening, arriving a little late, Fabien came in unannounced to the little room where we had our sessions. I was reading a book on the Tibetan language. He asked what it was, why I was doing it, whether it was homework, and if I had to do it. I replied that I was reading it for pleasure. He thought for a moment, realizing suddenly that I too had a life outside our weekly meetings, that we had separate lives, that each of us had a story that was ours alone. He talked about his own life, his school, and wanted to tell me about his work. He even said he would like me to do some grammar with him, since I was interested in language. But he would not ask me to do this now, he said, explaining in adult fashion that he had been working since early morning and had had enough for the day.

The conversation returned to the two of us. He calculated how long it had been since the beginning of his treatment. Memories came back to him, certain games, certain episodes, his anxiety about the teacher who had gone away, the dentist who had forbidden him to suck his thumb. He tried to recall the different rooms in the building in which we had met over the years and asked to see them again. I agreed, and we revisited the rooms together. In the corridor we passed one of the receptionists whom he knew well, as well as the doctor who had referred him to me. I could sense that Fabien was pleased to look back over the ground he had covered, but that there was also a certain sadness, no doubt linked with the inevitable sense of taking leave.

As we went back down the stairs to my office, he sang under his breath, 'Haul away, lads, at the windlass', and explained that this was a sea shanty. It was about somebody dying far from home, he said. I took up the words and sang with him, and let myself share with him a feeling that is difficult to describe. It was the prelude to separation, but at the same time it was an acknowledgement that we had been actors in the same story.

3

Kim: Seeking One's Own Language

More often than not a child's difficulties do not have their source in one single area. Broadly, Kim's problem was what is known as 'uncontrollable prolixity': she would sometimes begin talking a lot and without thinking. Here I shall explore how a particular situation may affect the way a problem is manifested and how that problem is affected by the presence of other people.

Kim on Screen

Kim was a little girl of 4½, born to a Cambodian father and

a Chinese mother. The family had fled to France to escape the Khmer Rouge camps, in which two older children in the family had already perished. The parents, who spoke Chinese to each other, spoke to Kim in French, Cambodian, or Chinese, but they could not understand what she said in any of these three languages. This is why they sought advice. My first encounter with her was an indirect one. I saw a video recording of a consultation with a doctor at the clinic. As I viewed the cassette I was struck by several things.

When the consulting doctor invited Kim to look into a box of toys and puppets she pointed at various things and named them in clear, comprehensible language. But that was where it ended. She touched none of the toys, began no activity, no game, no role play. The words she used showed that she had a certain vocabulary. But this added nothing to the exchange. She did not say what she was going to do or what she wanted. Nor did she use words to punctuate what had just happened. She simply named the things she saw to show that she was able to do it.

However, when Kim really did try to express herself, when she wanted to verbalize her thoughts, she ceased to speak correctly. What she said became unintelligible. She spoke her own private language. Yet her intonations gave the impression that the speech was coherent to her, even if it made no sense to her listeners. It was rather like a child who knows no English but mimics an American accent as he has heard it in a B-grade movie. The speech of this little girl was correct when it served no purpose beyond pointing and naming, but it disintegrated when she really wanted to express herself.

This strange inability to communicate was heightened by the fact that Kim seemed unable to grasp the meaning of suggestions made to her orally if she was not prepared for them.

Yet along with her obvious difficulties, she displayed unexpected talents. She made no mistakes when counting all the pieces in a collection while pointing at them. She could draw with astonishing skill. With three strokes of her pencil she could sketch the outline of the heroine of a cartoon, whom she called a *minette* (lit. 'kitten', idiomatic for '(little) girl'), or a man, or a dog. But as she did this she gave the impression of not knowing what she was trying to achieve. It was as if she were going through a routine of established motions, with no view of the whole. Sometimes, at the beginning, I copied her drawings in order to familiarize myself with the contours and to give Kim the feeling that, in one sense at least, I was able to follow her. She would usually give her drawings a decorative border, taking obvious pleasure in the sudden twists and turns of the lines. These looked like combed wave-crests on a rough sea. If I asked her to explain something to me she spoke in her jargon. I could understand nothing, but I could repeat it. When I repeated what she said, she nodded agreement.

The contrast between her difficulties and her talents left me wondering what position to adopt in the treatment. Should I help her to develop what she was spontaneously managing to do, and hope that the development would bring progress in the areas where she lagged behind? Or should I, on the contrary, put a brake on the elements that worked 'too well' so as to let her bring out whatever it was that had yet to fall into place? As will be seen, this was a false dichotomy. More important than this simplistic dilemma was the need to let her organize herself in the session. If she could define her rituals, her own space, the repetition could give way to a framework, a chronology capable of giving meaning to each event and forming expectations that Kim would be able to communicate to me.

In the video of that first consultation, another detail attracted my attention. When the consulting doctor asked, 'Where is your brother?' Kim replied by rotating both hands in front of her in a gesture associated with a traditional puppet song. The allusion to the song, which concludes 'trois petits tours et puis s'en vont' (three times round and off they go), as she put her hands behind her back, seemed to mean, 'My brother isn't here.' But why did Kim resort to a gesture rather than words? Why did she not say, 'Not here' or 'Gone', if she could say spontaneously 'cow', 'bull', or 'duck' when she saw the animals in the box? It was as if she were unable to speak when speech could serve some real purpose.

Having no answer to this I constructed a number of hypotheses. First, faced with the great variety of languages used around her, gesture may have seemed to her a way of nipping any misunderstanding in the bud. It was also possible that the consulting-room situation reminded her of school and that she adjusted to it by adopting a style of communication reminiscent of school and its rituals.

The way Kim used gestures was also noteworthy. When a child wishes to cope with separation in a game, it is rare to see any part of the body employed (except in hide-and-seek, when the whole body is engaged); the child tends to use some object, like the cotton reel in Freud's famous observations concerning his grandson, who hid things and then recovered them. Unlike Freud's grandson, Kim made use of her hands, hiding them or showing them like the cotton reel. But unlike the cotton reel, which would disappear under the bed, her hands, of course, remained firmly attached to her body even when hidden behind her back. Perhaps Kim's choice of her hands was a way of retaining a link with the missing object.

It is also possible that Kim's response in miming the actions of puppets was not really a sign. If we are to speak of signs proper, two conditions must be met. First, the object signified must be clearly delimited, and second, the subject must aim to communicate it to somebody. In this case it is difficult to tell if Kim had really grasped the logic of communication: her gestures indicated an association of ideas connected to an absence, rather than an answer in mime. The word 'brother', used by the consulting doctor, reminded her of the brother who was not present in the office. She then experienced a vague feeling of missing something and reacted by repeating a gesture also associated with a vague awareness of things that depart. French schoolchildren in the morning mime the puppet song 'trois petits tours et puis s'en vont' so as to forget their mothers' departure and their sudden loneliness on separation.

The turning and disappearing hands are symbolic of absence and make it possible to cope with the pain. But does this make them a sign?

Kim's gesture, which is also extremely rich in meaning, indicated that there was a serious obstacle in her language development. She did indeed use words to name animals, but, curiously, to express her wishes or her memories, she seemed to prefer using her hands. The whole symbolic effect of language was therefore inhibited.

First Meetings

The way in which the realignment of the division between the use of words and that of gestures began in our first sessions will help us understand how the symbolic and the cognitive had become intertwined.

Very early in the treatment, Kim showed that she knew how to organize our sessions according to a well-defined ritual. She quickly made herself at home, while I restricted myself to keeping her company and giving a rhythm to her actions. She habitually asked me to take out various things from the box of toys, starting with the toy fences. She would construct enclosures and put the animals inside. I did my best, using speech, to dramatize and orchestrate the way she set them out.

A second stage usually followed, in which I introduced a small element of conflict. Sometimes, for example, while showing her that I had perfectly understood what she wanted, I did not hurry to give it to her. This compelled her to use several different formulations to persuade me, all directed towards the thing that she wanted. This was a way of inducing her to return to the forward-looking function of language, while at the same time making her experience the fact that a referent is stable, although the linguistic signifiers that denote it may vary. Sometimes I merely suggested to her the name of a person or animal that figured in the preceding session but which now seemed to have been discarded. This reminder created a conflict that led her to say something to explain this omission. As a result she would complicate her arrangement, and this helped foster the development of a story.

To ensure that my suggestions produced constructive conflict, I had to take great care lest the tensions caused Kim to want to escape or retreat, as she sometimes did, into silent drawing. Moreover, the framework had to be sufficiently well established: Kim had to know what was going on, be assured that our attention was fixed on the same object of thought, and know that the rules governing the sequence of our exchanges were stable. When all went well and Kim constructed the scenario of the session without too many disruptions, she was obliged at each stage to make a choice from a range of options, each of which excluded all the others. Each time the options were limited to a number of simple and well-defined actions. If, for example, she had just constructed an enclosure, she had the choice of putting an animal in it or of building another enclosure next to it and leaving the first one empty. Given the repetition, the limited choice of actions permitted Kim to have a definite thought in her mind even if she still lacked the words to express it. Now that things were clear to her—or now that I could suppose that they were clear—it was possible for me to modify the game in ways that would make sense to her, even if the suggestion deflected her from her habits.

The first time I met Kim she was accompanied by her mother and a social worker from the team that had referred her to me.

Kim entered the room, made straight for the whiteboard, and drew some clouds. Then she added a mass of little dots beneath them, representing raindrops, with extremely repetitive motions that she seemed not to wish to interrupt. I let her find her bearings. After a while, as time seemed to be slipping away, I pointed to a space where she had as yet made no mark, and said 'there'. Then I took a marker pen and placed a little dot at that precise point. She looked at me in silence, with a mixture of interest and vague annoyance. I said, 'Your turn.' She grasped the idea at once and indicated another empty space, saying, 'There', and marking a dot in it. Alternation was progressively established according to this pattern. Then it changed. I indicated a space, and she marked the dot. Finally, we exchanged roles.

In this game our attention and our interest were jointly focused on an area of empty space, a space where there was still no dot. This meeting-point of interests, slender though it was, demonstrated the existence of some common ground in our dialogue. The game continued in this way for a while, before I complicated it again by drawing circles, squares, and triangles. As Kim could name each shape without hesitation, I permitted myself to point to a space and suggested, 'A circle?', and let her draw a circle. Then the roles were reversed again: she said, 'Triangle?' and I drew the figure.

In this exchange, Kim's use of language returned to normal. The word did not duplicate the presence of the object; it anticipated its presence. The orders we gave each other expressed a plan. We were not naming a shape that was present on the board, but foreshadowing a movement and a mark.

During our second session, Kim noticed some Russian matrioshka dolls on my desk. In themselves, these dolls seem to me to have a particular quality, at the junction of two ways of apprehending the world of games. On the one hand, their shape and regularity suggest inclusion and nesting clusters, and on the other, comparisons of size and arrangement in series. In brief, these dolls suggest a range of abstract manipulations that call to mind those that the followers of Piaget studied in child development. But also, as one looks at these 'little women', one cannot fail to think of all the babies hidden inside them and the way they can symbolize successive generations emerging from them.

As Kim did not appear eager to handle the dolls spontaneously, I opened the first one, then the second, then the third, hoping that she would join in. But she was content to look at the open dolls. I said to her, 'You can open one.' Was it my tone of voice or the suggestion itself that activated her? This time she picked up the next doll, the last, and opened it.

All the open pieces were lined up, out of sequence, on the table in front of her, and she set about reassembling them. She picked up the top half of the biggest matrioshka and looked for the matching bottom half. It was there in front of her, but at the far end of the table. When she began this exercise she had not yet noticed it. Slowly she looked over the range of bottom halves, comparing their size with the mental image of the one she wanted to match with the top half of the doll she was holding. Each time the test was negative and she proceeded to inspect the next piece. Her procedure was meticulous, methodical, and determined, and in view of the rigour she was applying I expected her to complete the process without much difficulty. But with two dolls to go Kim abandoned the task and lost interest in the search. She dropped it, as if tired by the complexity of the undertaking.

As I watched her at work I realized that the process of comparison was quite complex. It relied upon establishing a connection between an actual perception—the bottom half which she had before her—and a mental image, the image of the matching upper half, which she had formed from her perception of the bottom half. It seemed to me that Kim's weariness resulted from the fact that she was unable to retain a sufficiently clear mental image. Unless it was restored regularly by actual perception of the matching segment, it became blurred in her mind after a series of comparisons.

Yet, when I showed her the piece she wanted at the end of the row, she recognized it at once and proceeded to assemble the doll.

A little later in the session an analogous phenomenon arose. In our box of toys she found a tea-set and tried to collect all the spoons. I noticed one last spoon on the table, hidden behind the box, next to a little lion that was also hidden from her. I said to her, without pointing, 'There's another spoon next to the lion.' She drew near, leaned over the box and saw the lion. The sight of this figure no doubt reassured her that the word I had used was indeed 'lion'. She was about to pick up the lion. But when she noticed the spoon she remembered her original intention and picked it up instead of the lion.

Here again, the actual perception of an object had dimmed the mental image which had guided her movements up to this point, and almost deflected her from her purpose. Perhaps also because it figured in my oral directions, the lion distracted her for a moment from her wish to find the spoon.

Slight Disruptions

During the next session Kim returned to the Russian dolls. This time she opened them with precision, showing that she had absorbed very well what had transpired the previous week. She arranged the figures in descending order of size, then set about inserting them inside one another in a very systematic manner: first she tackled only the bottom halves, which she placed one inside the other, then she attached the top halves, from the smallest to the largest. Like all children, she took the largest top, looked at the series, found the largest bottom, reassembled the largest doll, then realized that a lot of tops remained outside. She was then obliged to undo what she had just done, in order to complete the series. She corrected her mistake each time.

As the cycle of attempts, false starts, and reassembly was repeated endlessly, I wanted to introduce a disruption. At a point in between two games, when she had lined up all the dolls in order of size, I took a medium-sized doll and put it behind a cushion, as she watched. Curiously, Kim looked on without paying attention to my action. She did not try to reclaim the doll I had taken from her, but continued to play as if nothing had happened. She pulled each of the dolls apart and set about reassembling them, again starting by slowly and diligently fitting the bottoms inside one another. When, however, she reached the size of the one which I had taken she realized that something was missing. She then paused and went to recover the doll under the cushion.

An incident which at the time seemed insignificant took on meaning later. When I hid the doll, my action held no meaning for Kim as she could not yet visualize a need for it. Later the gap left by the missing doll became an anomaly and called for action to regularize the series. At this point the 'snapshot' she had taken of my movement, although she had lent it no significance, supplied what was needed to even out the anomaly, and she went to recover the doll concealed under the cushion.

It may seem paradoxical that this child, who in the previous session was unable to make the comparison between a mental picture and an object before her eyes, could now analyse the current situation to find a clue to a missing object, and then go and fetch it. We might be tempted to think that it is simpler to locate the desired piece when it is standing fully visible in a row of dolls than to go and get it from under a cushion, having deduced its absence from an analysis of the situation.

A number of hypotheses may explain Kim's reaction. First, the initial scene—the search for the correct bottom half in the series—depended on an act of serial comparison between the mental image of the object sought and the various objects present before her eyes. By contrast, in the process that provides the impulse for Kim to look under the cushion there is only one operation, which consists of connecting the interruption in the series of reinserted bottom halves with the event of concealment. The first comparison calls forth a sequence of virtual representations of the half-doll being sought. In the latter case, a glance suffices to confirm that something is missing.

But we may also conjecture that Kim was not simply going to fetch the missing piece in the series, but was seeking the object I had hidden, which happened to be a doll. In other words, the interruption did not simply return her to the mental image of a half-doll defined by size, but to an incident that occurred in the relationship she and I had established. The task was therefore enriched by the fact that it was not a question of a simple cognitive search but of one motivated by the activation of the totality of the relationship. Put another way, for Kim it was not simply a case of locating a missing piece in a series but of recovering something that I had made a show of concealing from her, and of responding to my trick and gaining the upper hand. The realms of emotion and play lent support and meaning to the realm of cognition. The *symbolic* dimension could now develop.

This episode was all the more important for the fact that it led to a shift of levels within a session. Shortly after she had recovered the doll, Kim abandoned this game and turned again to the toy box. As in the previous session, she first took some fences and built a pen, in which she placed the animals. I let her continue her game until at a certain moment I picked up a dog—a St Bernard with a barrel on its collar—and put it outside the pen with its front paws resting on a fence. Without giving the matter much thought, I was placing it at the boundary of the two worlds circumscribed by Kim, as if to re-establish a link between the inside and the outside. Kim then took hold of all the biting animals, as well as various horned animals, and attacked the dog. This was the first time she had taken an initiative of this kind. No doubt this aggressive action directed against me was in response to my hiding the Russian doll, as well as to the fact that the dog, both inside and outside, represented a provocative intrusion into the space she had just delimited. As the biting game seemed set to continue, I decided to protect the dog by moving it a little to the side and placing some more fences in front of it. Changing sides, Kim then took hold of the dog and set about making it systematically bite all the animals that had attacked it. The defences I had set up seemed to enable Kim to enrich her symbolic action by identifying with me and making the animal I had protected react.

In the development of this session, the realignment of Kim's games seems to me critical. The pleasure of the first scene with the Russian dolls came from the solitary exercise of cognitive powers. Kim enjoyed packing and unpacking containers that had to be arranged in series, and comparing them to one another. But as soon as the question of absence arises, with the episode of the doll hidden under the cushion, as soon as her search for the missing object brings back an emotional memory of what had passed between us, the impulse changes. The discovery of the doll assumes a symbolic value which opens the way to new games in which the imagination has a place. Now the episode with the animals that bite or fence themselves in can follow. The transition from the cognitive (which sees nothing of the matrioshka beyond its physically perceptible features and dimensions) to the symbolic (in which the matrioshka can be seen as representing an exchange between us) leads us into the familiar world of child psychotherapy. No doubt, for Kim to be able to work in this way, the thing being thought of had to be absent in order to be detached from the physical reality and become represented.

Up to this point, although I could see that Kim had perceptibly changed, she had not spoken. It was only during the next session that she really began to use language.

During this session she started taking the fences and arranging them in a square, clearly wishing to place the animals inside. But I kept the box on my lap and did not let her see what was in it, while inviting her to ask me what she wanted. She then named from memory all the animals she had played with the time before, starting with the pair formed by the cow and the bull. All were named, one after the other, except for the crocodile and the hippopotamus. I wondered about this omission. Was it because their names were difficult to pronounce, or did she simply leave out those that can bite the hardest?

Kim then busied herself with the animal enclosures. She changed their arrangement to form gateways under which all the animals had to pass, except the lion, who was permitted to jump over them. It was while she was playing this new game that she began to speak. While placing the animals, she named the positions in which she was putting them: 'inside–outside' or 'above–below'. The naming of these positions was accompanied by the actions. Then, when she had finished, she gave a thumbs-up sign to show me she was satisfied. This gesture, offered in lieu of some exclamation such as 'super!', recalled the hand-turning of the puppets. The thumbs-up gesture did not serve to demonstrate or mime anything. It was purely to communicate a feeling, an emotional state.

At the end of our session, at the moment when we shook hands, Kim said to me clearly, 'Till next time!' I had not expected this and was quite touched by her way of looking forward to our next meeting, demonstrating that she could think of separation and—this time—express it in words (even if the words were still bound up with the ritual of the handshake). By saying 'Till next time!' Kim was supplying a word which referred to our current situation and anticipated our next meeting, so exhibiting the emergence of a new sense of time.

The Exchange with Kim, and her Misunderstandings

In our early sessions Kim's language did not develop greatly but there was a certain shift in her way of using words. Before considering how the written word helped her to make a real leap forward, I would like to pause for a moment on her way of communicating.

The anxiety and linguistic confusion that reigned in this refugee family would suffice, no doubt, to account for Kim's use of hand gestures to express herself. But her self-expression and comprehension were essentially blocked by the fact that the mechanism of language was not in place. Throughout our sessions (and even today), Kim had difficulty in understanding what was said to her when one broached a new subject.

During everyday exchanges, dialogue presupposes some mental accord that permits the speakers to direct their attention in the same direction. Most misunderstandings arise from a failure to establish this common ground. When one knows a language well, the first words of a conversation immediately suffice to establish a context for the total exchange. We may not know what the other speaker is going to say, but we anticipate in broad terms the subject they will speak of and the viewpoint likely to be adopted. But when our knowledge of a language is incomplete, recourse to gestures is indispensable (we become aware of this difficulty when we have to communicate by telephone in an unfamiliar language). In the same way, either because they cannot identify accurately the sound contours of the word they hear, or because the word once recognized does not evoke any particular area of meaning, some children—and some adults—experience difficulty in establishing the common ground of discourse from purely linguistic information.

This was where Kim's difficulties of comprehension lay. When unprepared for the situation, if she and I had not determined our theme in advance, the words she heard were not enough for her to perform the required delimitation of the field. If my words could not be fitted into a definite framework, they had no meaning for her. But, when the situation provided a framework, her faculty of comprehension could operate again.

During our second session, for example, while we were playing with the Russian dolls, Kim understood my suggestion, 'You can open the little one, you know,' because I was opening the first dolls before her eyes. My actions gave us a shared focus. But if she had a box in front of her and I said, 'Open the box,' she seemed to neither hear nor understand. She ignored my words. I had to point to the box; then her face brightened and she reacted to my invitation to lift the lid. Pointing was not simply a way of indicating the object to be handled. It assured her that I was indeed speaking to her of a 'box' and enabled her to frame a whole field of vocabulary.

If I then uttered words such as 'open', 'close', 'inside', 'lid', etc., the restriction placed on the field by pointing reassured her in her understanding and enabled her to recognize and interpret the words I was using.

At times, Kim's difficulties in understanding had more harmful effects. This was evident not in her silence but in her inappropriate responses. For instance, during one session we were playing with cutlery and I had all the available spoons in my hand. I asked her if she would give me a knife. She shook her head vigorously: 'No.' It was clear that she was not refusing to give me a knife. She simply thought that I was asking for another spoon to complete my collection. Since she knew that there were no more spoons she said 'No' to inform me that she could not give me any more. The spoons which she could see in my hand led her to think that I was speaking of spoons and this deduction prevailed over what she had actually heard.

On another occasion she wanted a fence that I was holding in my hand, and as she tried to wrest it from me I suggested that she say to me, 'If you want it, tell me to let go.' At once Kim relaxed her grip and let go of the fence. She had interpreted the words 'let go' as an order and dissociated them from the rest of my sentence.

One Meaning per Word

Kim's difficulty in accepting a theme suggested by somebody else had a number of consequences. The brittle bossiness that she often displayed in our exchanges no doubt had much to do with it. As she imperfectly understood what I meant, she tried to uphold her own point of view because there, at least, she knew where she was. This stubbornness was linked with her difficulties in changing course while following the speech of another person, and this lent her an air of obstinacy and being out of her depth. Kim would seek to impose her way of seeing things, loath to allow any suggestion from me of what she might propose and always sticking to her own idea. But if I showed the slightest firmness in my own suggestions, she would abandon her original notion, as if her obduracy were shattered when it came up against my opposition.

There was another consequence: she took particular care to assign no more than one meaning to each word. If I exclaimed 'Well done!' (*Chapeau!*, lit. 'hat'), instead of 'Bravo!', to express my approval, she would reply, 'No, not hat!' She could identify the word perfectly well, but since nothing in the situation actually had any connection with a hat she would not admit the use of the word. Each word should have one fixed meaning. We might wonder what it was that caused her to react to the word 'hat'. From the point of view of the manner of expression, the word is an exclamation that stands out sharply from the rest of our discourse. As a signifier, it is strongly highlighted by intonation. Moreover, my intonation and facial expression were sufficient to show Kim that I wished to express my approval. Finally, she knew what a hat was. Being well aware of these three elements, she felt that the word did not correspond to the reality to which I was applying it. But, being unable to re-evaluate its meaning in terms of our particular situation, she rejected it. In short, she was not sufficiently sure of what she knew to let herself be distracted from it when she encountered something unforeseen. For her, a word could have only one referent, and must stand in a monovalent relationship with the situation. For any new meaning a new word was required.

This quest for monovalence could be seen in her manner of drawing. Like all children, she sometimes wanted to cancel a sketch she had just made by crossing it out. But to do this, Kim would take her pencil in her other hand, as if her changed view of her drawing obliged her to break her ties with herself, as if the negative opinion were someone else's and she were thus the arena for two juxtaposed impulses: the wish to make the drawing, expressed by one hand, and the wish to cancel it, expressed by the other in the form of the crossed lines. There is no doubt that she was not doing this deliberately. It was a purely mechanical action. But it showed the difficulty Kim had in expressing two opposed points of view. She could not link together her wish to make a drawing and her rejection of that drawing. Hence the curious division of the two actions between her two hands.

Jargon and its Limits

In her speech Kim sometimes resorted to words that were purely her own, especially when she commented on a drawing she had just produced. Several times she would speak of a 'gontru', which seemed to mean 'thingummy'; but each time I said, 'Ah! It's a thingummy, is it?' she would shake her head vigorously. This kind of expression recalls what studies of aphasia term 'jargonaphasia', a form of utterance in which the subject pronounces non-existent words owing to an inability to model the sounds he produces on an auditory memory of familiar signifiers. But this jargon has variable manifestations. Not all Kim's words are garbled and it is not the longest or most complex of them that are worst pronounced. To signal exasperation and contradiction, she would exclaim, 'What-non-sense!'. In a purely automatic way, her bad temper thus found expression in a linguistically correct form.

Similarly, Kim could count objects up to ten and beyond without error and enunciate the French words for 'triangle', 'rectangle', and 'square' perfectly. In these cases, her surprising verbal precision was due to the fact that the pronunciation of each word was framed by an accompanying action. The names of geometric figures were linked with the movements involved in drawing those figures, and the names of the numbers were linked with the ritual motions of counting (such as taking items from a pile and placing them beside one).

No doubt the special role of motor functions for Kim also explained the early appearance of terms denoting spatial location. For example, while she had great difficulty in saying the word 'barrière', she was fully able to explain that the lion was next to the pig by saying 'à côté cochon' (for 'à côté du cochon'). Similarly, after playing at changing the places of certain animals in different enclosures, she accompanied the gestures with 'It's not my place', meaning that the animals were not where they should be. Her command of spatial location terms was well ahead of the rest of her vocabulary because all localization could be construed as the end point of a hand movement.

Word and Action

Briefly stated, Kim's preference for movement rather than feeling determined her verbalization. A word came to life in her memory not because it reminded her of any sensations which might attach to it, but because it reminded her of certain actions of which it had happened to be the instrument. In order to find the name of an object via the action associated with it we must be able to touch or at least see it. We have seen how much more at ease Kim was when trying to name objects she could see than when asking for others that she wanted but could not see. But indirectly, her enforced reliance on things being present inverted the natural use of language. Since words could not help her to designate people or things not present, she preferred to rely on gestures, as in the episode of the puppetlike hand movements.

After several sessions, Kim managed to ask me for some animals that were still in the box, and thus hidden from view. Later still, on seeing that one of the Russian dolls lacked its top half, she would say, for example: 'It's missing,' or, while pointing to an enclosure from which she had taken all the animals, she would exclaim, 'They aren't there!' At such moments the relation between the word, the object, and its representation was organized in the proper order.

Although Kim managed increasingly to verbalize what was absent in a given situation, the natural relation between the word and the missing object still did not seem to have been fully established. I shall attempt to demonstrate this by a few examples, beginning with our game. For some time, to show me that she wanted a fence, Kim would go through the motion of marking a division between two groups of animals and saying, 'Un ça' (A that). It is true that she was showing me what she would use the fence for. But her gesture also gave firm shape to the division that the fences, if present, would have enabled her to mark: it follows, then, that real fences were no longer indispensable and seemed to be only a superfluous addition to the space marked between the animals. I am therefore tempted to say that Kim's words and gestures did not bear quite the same relation to the objects they designated. Her gesture did not invoke an idea; it prepared the reality to receive what was lacking. This was why the object itself had less importance once the gesture had been made.

In addition, Kim sometimes played with some missing element as if it were present. One day she used the fences to construct a series of enclosures. Each one was a pen in which she placed a single animal. After a while she withdrew all the fences, leaving the animals in spaces that no longer had anything to mark their limits. But from the way she moved the animals it seemed as if the fences were still in position. For Kim, what constituted an enclosure was not a visible structure but the act of assembling one. Removal of the barriers did not mean cancelling the separation. With almost any other child, removing the barriers would have meant starting an immediate fight between the animals. Not with Kim.

Another curious consequence flowed from her mental treatment of absence. In the toybox there was a toy that originally consisted of three ducks in single file attached to the same base. The middle duck had been torn off. Only the impressions of its feet remained on the base. Kim had never seen this toy intact, yet when holding it she would say, 'Ducks, three', as if it were immaterial to her that the middle one was missing. I do not believe she was unaware that it was missing. Rather I believe that her way of saying 'three ducks' shows that she was not counting objects but the number of times she should say the word 'duck'. She should say 'duck' twice for the two ducks present, and once more for the place where the trace of a duck remained on the base. Since the same word designated the missing duck and the two visible ducks, she counted a total of 'three ducks'. Thus she tended to accord the same status to a missing duck as to one that was present.

The Written Word

I now come to an important moment in Kim's language development. I have already mentioned Kim's interest in drawing, her rapid sketches of stylized young girls which resembled Japanese cartoon figures. But what was even more surprising was her interest in writing. I must confess to being stunned when she tried to spell out 'z-o-o' to make me see the meaning of the way she had arranged the fences on the table. When she did the same with the name of an animal I resolved to take the matter further.

I brought to one of our sessions a small picture dictionary that showed various objects with their names in big letters at the foot of the page. The pictures were not so much educational as an appeal to the imagination and the emotions. I opened the book and as I turned the pages I read out the name of the thing depicted, then wrote the word myself. Kim listened with interest. Then we reversed our roles. Kim wrote, copying from the book, and I deciphered what she wrote as she took it down. In the next session Kim had made a spectacular leap in her use of language.

I shall attempt to find some possible causes for this leap. First, it seems to me that the presence of a picture reassured Kim that both of us were thinking of the same thing at the same time. This assurance freed her from her lack of confidence in matters of language. Moreover, we have seen that actions assisted her production of words. We may recall that during our first sessions the sight of an object seemed to prompt some action related to the object, and that this action in turn prompted her to enunciate something. This time it was no longer a question of an action linked to an object, but of a hand movement that enabled her to write the name of the object. The movement of the wrist and the mark left on the paper seemed to provide Kim with the syllables she lacked. In other words, the movement of the pencil as it marked out the syllables provided support for the movements which enabled her mouth to pronounce them. What is more, it must be said that Kim, who was barely able to speak, had a more highly developed sense of correct spelling than the author of these lines. Opening the dictionary at our next session, I showed her a picture of a twelfth-night cake with a crown on it. The only word written was 'cake'. As I showed her the crown and pronounced the word, she asked me to write it. Unfortunately I misspelt the word for 'crown', *couronne*, giving it only one n. As soon as I had done so, she pointed to my mistake, clearly vexed: 'That's not right', she said reproachfully. Since she was right, I corrected my error.

Thus, the motion of tracing the letters on a sheet of paper provided an intermediate link that enabled Kim to arrive at the correct pronunciation—without her private jargon—of words. In the treatment of aphasia, writing frequently affords substantial support to the spoken language. The emphasis that Kim spontaneously gave to gesture and action allowed her to find reassurance in letters and their written shapes.

What then was the basic nature of Kim's language problem? When asked to repeat a word or series of words, she did so at once. On the other hand, she did not always succeed in articulating sounds in the sequence required to pronounce words correctly. Yet if her memory of the pronunciation of words was faulty, that of the act of writing did not pose the same problem. So, in order to find actions that would enable her to pronounce a syllable, she would rely on the shape of the letters as she wrote them. In this way the words could more easily be called to mind.

When Books Release Language

For several sessions we used the illustrated glossary. After a while, seeking to avoid repetition, I placed the book out of Kim's reach. She spontaneously returned to two earlier games. She asked me for the little figures of the dog and the crocodile. However, in spite of a certain amount of repetition, I was surprised to see that her games had developed. Between the dog and the crocodile she organized a form of activity involving disappearance and reappearance. This was a kind of hide-and-seek during which one of the animals ambushed the other and then hid under the table (she accompanied this with the words 'It's hidden') out of sight of the other. Suddenly the notion of presence and absence appeared in her games. Moments later, she took the box lid and used it as a pond in which the animals could paddle. Then she picked up the ducks again, this time stating the actual number of ducks remaining: 'Ducks, two ducks.' Then, pointing to each of the ducks on the stand, she tried to mark the place of the missing one, saying: 'One broken, two not broken.' She did not say 'It's gone' of the missing one, and in her description 'broken' was a feature of a duck that she appeared to see. Thus her statement of the absence of the third duck was still less than fully formulated. But when compared to the earlier sessions, before we began reading, something had changed as she no longer said 'three ducks' while looking at the stand.

Her game with death was also quick to develop. One morning the lion and the monkey had a fight. The lion killed the monkey. She took hold of the monkey and said, 'The monkey's dead'. A moment later she exclaimed 'monkey!' in a louder voice. This overdetermined exclamation was a kind of resurrection, invoking all that the monkey represented for her. A way of addressing it in order to convince herself that it was in fact alive, or of informing me that she was 'cancelling' its death. After this exclamation she took the monkey and reintroduced it into her game. She reversed, cancelled, overturned the progression and started again. The monkey hid and the dog looked for it. One of them leapt out and surprised the other—as she herself had done many times when going out to meet her mother after a session, springing out at the last moment from behind the door into the corridor to startle her. But in her games with the animals on the box lid, Kim was no longer content to be an actor; she was now director as well.

I watched her at play and reflected on the range of meanings contained in her activity. Her games of hide-and-seek were clearly not intended only to cope with separation, but to take somebody by surprise and show that it is possible to be alive, to exist where one might not be expected to: 'I exist even if you're not looking, even if you're not thinking of me,' is the message expressed by the one that jumps out at the other. By miming this scene, played out not only with her mother now, but between the animals, on a stage, with me looking on, Kim was showing how much she had changed.

And when she left the room she no longer said, 'Till next time!' She could imagine separation without having to attach her thoughts immediately to the next meeting. From now on she was able to find within herself the resources to continue existing even when nobody was looking.

A *Closing Session*

In conclusion I would like to convey the tenor of one of our last sessions.

Kim went to the drawing-board and drew a story of boats in several episodes. Curiously, the different stages of this story appeared side by side on the same sheet. When a character changed his position she drew him twice, in each of his positions. Thus time was levelled, just as the difference between presence and absence was levelled in the case of the ducks.

She completed the drawing with a departure scene.

L.D.-B.: It's a sailing boat. So who's on it?
KIM: It's Monsieur Boileau.

As she said this she started drawing again, and added a very clear figure at the stern of the boat.

L.D.-B.: And what else is there?

She made no reply but started drawing some pretty wave crests on the sea. Suddenly a huge whale surfaced; two large jets of water spurted skyward from its nostrils and fell back. Below the whale, Kim drew the shape of an artillery shell, about which she said nothing.

Then, still saying nothing, she went on drawing on the same

page. In the next stage the whale, now a terrifying beast, was devouring the man and the boat.

In one corner of the drawing was the sun, with two eyes and a mouth. It wore a slightly mocking expression. A little way off there was another whale, a small one.

Throughout, when I asked what it was all about, she would explain in some detail and in perfectly comprehensible fashion. I asked whether the sails of the boats were at such a steep angle because of a strong wind or because they were sampans.

She took a fresh sheet and continued her story. In one of the boats a little girl appeared with a knife. A whale surfaced. She threw a sort of harpoon. On the end of the harpoon Kim drew the whale again, on its side at the bottom of the sea. 'It's dead,' she explained. Then the sun had a harpoon too and it joined the little girl's harpoon in the body of the whale. Now there was a new twist to the story: a little boy with short hair and no legs appeared. At his side was a little girl with long hair and a skirt. Both were holding knives. Then Kim gave them each a fork and a spoon so that they could eat the whale. Kim signed her name and ended the story with the words 'The End'.

With this story in pictures Kim departed in spectacular fashion from the repetitive and kindergarten drawing style that she had adhered to when she spoke little. Now, as she began to speak, her personal artistic output exploded, giving me cause for personal alarm in the process...

4
Rachid:
Word and Gesture

Difficulties in language development sometimes have short-term consequences for the thought processes of a child. Certain cognitive problems may have similar effects. We know, for example, that autistic children have difficulty in interpreting the meaning of other people's body language and facial expressions, and it is now thought that the ability to do this is partly innate.

Here I shall deal with a particular type of cognitive imbalance. We might illustrate it with a picture by an artist who is less interested in the end product than in hand and brush movements on the canvas, an artist who sees the act of painting as more important than the result. In some ways, Rachid resembles this imaginary artist.

First Impressions

When I first saw him, Rachid was a slightly peculiar child. He seemed disinclined to play. At the age of nearly 4, he did not use language to communicate. He could, however, read numbers consisting of several digits and count objects up to twelve, as well as write some letters of the alphabet. When alone, he would move his fingers about in endless intricate patterns, sometimes chanting to himself in strings of incomprehensible words. He did not seem actually to avoid contact, but the hand he extended to greet me seemed light, frail, and almost absent. When he entered my office, the first thing he often did was to go to the drawing-board and run a red felt-tip marker methodically round the inner edge of the aluminium frame, drawing a frame within the frame, rising as high as he could reach, with great regularity. Autistic? I would not say so, since although he displayed signs that are sometimes associated with autism, such as this finger gestures, there was some interchange. One could share things with Rachid that would have been impossible to share with an autistic child, even if the interchange was fragile and sometimes broke off. Moreover, the act of running a felt-tip round the whiteboard frame was not simply a ritualistic way of calming the anxiety caused by being shut in the room with me. The rectangular frame also resembled a television set. And Rachid was very fond of television.

Although often absorbed in his own movements, Rachid remained open to other people, and when playing he showed that he retained certain memories. I often felt that he tended to be somewhat unfocused. It seemed as if the enveloping embrace of somebody's gaze was needed for the events of his life to be shaped into a story. This thought came to me when I noticed that his mother would avert her eyes when she said goodbye to me. I thought of this again later, when she mentioned the early death of one of Rachid's playmates, of whom Rachid often spoke.

Today, approximately one year after the beginning of his treatment, Rachid speaks. He also does much more drawing, but in his drawings one can see something of our earlier encounters. For example, he continues to prefer drawing doors and windows to people. He also retains a taste for frames and lines that help to divide space. This seems to be something that will endure.

In our early sessions I would observe him with little understanding. In one of our offices, Rachid noticed a board game, though it was not in the foreground of his vision, and found in it two dice, which he rolled. One turned up a six and the other a five. He immediately read 'sixty-five', then went to the board and meticulously wrote a line of numbers. He changed colours for every new figure. First he named the colour he intended to use, then picked up the new felt-tip pen, wrote the numeral, replaced the cap, took another, and so on. A few moments later a luminous call number used in the clinic to signal therapists lit up above the door. It consisted of three digits: a five, a zero and a five. Rachid at once read this as 'five hundred and five'. He knew that five–zero–five was read differently from five–five–zero. Returning to the dice, he suggested a game in which I had to throw the same total as his. During this session his mother was present. We took turns with the dice. Rachid called out our turns: 'Mummy's go,' 'Monsieur Laurent's go,' 'Rachid's go'.

At first, the greater part of our time was spent on counting, ordering, stocktaking, and enumerating exhaustively all the components of every kind of combination of things. Rachid's taste for the comprehensive ran to innumerable inventories, including the colours and names of the wooden animals that I gave him to play with. This pleasure, incidentally, was one that he was eager to share with me as soon as possible, enjoining me to be the recorder of his endless lists: lists of things to eat (chocolate buns, *petit-suisse*, garden peas, etc.), abbreviations culled from television (*quarté-plus*, a system of betting on four horses; M6, a television network for children, A2, Antenne Deux, a television station), which I had to write on the board before his vigilant eye. If I happened to omit the final s of 'garden peas' he asked me to correct my error, pointing it out to me sharply. Sometimes he would ask me to write his name on the board, then the names of his mother, father, little brother, and sometimes my own, as 'Monsieur Laurent'. It was the letters that he liked. If I wanted to draw a man he would turn away and start counting, or go to the window, lift the curtain and say 'cars', as he looked out at the cars in the street.

A little later, however, drawing became acceptable. Rachid seemed to want to draw. He went so far as to pick up a pencil himself. Then, naming each thing as he drew it, he sketched a nose, a mouth, eyes, arms, and legs. On paper all these things were in place, and yet they did not add up to a real picture. To Rachid, drawing meant moving meticulously through a series of coded actions: it was the gestures that claimed his attention, not the result. And what was left on the paper as a 'drawing' was often a collection of fragments suspended in a void: eyes and a mouth without the outline of a head.

Fragmented Thought

Paradoxically, while Rachid had an uncommon gift for figures and letters, he seemed to have great difficulty in linking certain shapes together, especially a curve with a straight line. This meant he could not produce a d or a b because it was necessary to connect a rounded body with a vertical stroke. He also had difficulty forming a 3, and to make an M he would start at the top of the right leg, form a V by working back towards himself, then add the left leg before completing the letter with the right leg. As for curved and wavy lines and curlicues of any kind, he never produced any, at least not in the first six months of our treatment. He also seemed to have great difficulty in completing a drawing that was not his. For instance, one day, when he wished to redden the lips of a face that I had drawn at his request, he took the red felt-tip, clearly named 'the lips', and was about to colour in the outline of the mouth. But having taken the pen from me he did no more than mark a crude cross beside the drawing, as if he had seen what needed to be done, but the act of taking the pen had caused him to forget the intended action.

Rachid's difficulties with drawing resurfaced when he tried to interpret drawings done by others. One day he asked me to draw all the members of his family, distinguishing them by specific details: a cigarette in his father's mouth and a pony-tail on his mother's head. Each time he indicated to me the place where I must draw in his additions. For his father I drew the cigarette, then added the personal touch of a wisp of smoke rising vertically from it. At this, Rachid became cross and said, 'No, no hair.' He seemed to have taken my lines indicating smoke for hair. The smoke was curly, it is true, like hair, but this interpretation took no account of the position of the lines in the picture.

In my view, these varied reactions had a common cause in the fact that, in producing and interpreting signs, Rachid focused on the action itself. He took my wisp of smoke for hair because he retained nothing of the line beyond the twisting motion involved in producing it. Its place in the finished sketch was irrelevant. For it to be relevant, he would have had to show some interest in the product, the finished drawing of the man.

Employing symbols means making use of some perceptible material element in order to share a thought, that is, an abstraction, with another person. From this perspective, the act of drawing itself is the use of symbols. To sketch a 'little man with a big head' is to try to represent in symbolic fashion a person whom one cannot see. But what remains of symbolic value when, as in Rachid's case, the drawing displays such a bias towards the act of producing it? What is being represented when the most important thing is not the result but the series of movements made by the hand holding the pencil? This is what I would now like to consider by way of different contextual situations, some of which have nothing to do with drawing.

Early in our work, Rachid chanced upon the glove-puppet of a cat in our box of toys. He put his hand into it and mimed the action of soaping his face, as if he were wearing a wash-mitt, paying no heed whatever to the actual form of the puppet. How are we to interpret this action? For Rachid, the puppet is not a representation of a cat but a pocket of fabric into which one can insert one's hand, as one does into a wash-mitt to wash one's face. And if he cannot see the puppet as a substitute for a cat, it is because the signs suggest actions to him above all. A glove suggests a very simple action, but it does not suggest a cat. Of course, one might think of stroking a cat-puppet, or of hitting it. But in order for this to happen there must first be an imaginary scenario in which the puppet has ceased to be a piece of fabric. A hammer directly evokes the utilitarian action of hammering, and a wash-mitt that of washing. A cat puppet does nothing of the kind. In my view, this is the obstacle that Rachid came up against: in order to either stroke or hit this puppet he would have needed to be able to conjure up a whole scenario including some kind of relationship with a nice cat or an ill-natured cat. It was not the memory of actions that caused problems for Rachid; he was perfectly capable of going through the motions of rubbing the puppet on his arm like a wash-mitt. What was difficult was integrating this action into an overall context. For example, in the episode of the red lips, there is no doubt that his difficulty lay not in colouring in that part of the area corresponding to the lips, but rather in seeing in this action some significance relating to my drawing of a man. Rachid was unable to execute a precise movement when it was necessary to place it within something larger that would lend it some meaning. He had trouble linking different registers of thought and integrating them within a symbolic process. On the other hand, the recollection of the action proper was easy for him.

Once having performed the action, Rachid was able to use it as the basis of an imagined scenario. His use of the puppet as a wash-mitt underlined a difficulty in conjuring up an imaginary cat, but it was also a way of showing that it was possible to think of a bath scene with its array of visual, emotional, and motor associations. The problem was that Rachid took excessive pleasure in the motions themselves, which partially distracted him from the product of the motions. Hence the endless repetition, in one session after another, of observing some ritual that often eluded me. I did not find this tedious, as a slightly disturbing feeling of astonishment kept me on the alert. My varied reading had convinced me that a fragmented perception could sometimes form a starting point. I hoped that all this would assume some shape and grow in the course of our association.

Games and Absence

Although Rachid's games were fairly repetitive for a long time, at least they were there and there was some development. It was not so much the repetition that distinguished his games from those of other children, but rather some almost imperceptible features which I will try to elaborate. One day I saw Rachid in the waiting-room with a doll's house that looked like a prefabricated house. He was playing with the sliding door of the garage. When I came in he showed me how it opened, saying 'Metro'. He was pleased with this game, and it was not the activity alone that engaged his attention, but also the connection he could see between the things he was handling at that moment and what the Metro represented to him. One might suppose that, unlike Kim, who indicated her brother's absence by using her hands rather than any object, Rachid had found an equivalent to the cotton-reel game described by Freud.

Except that he had replaced the opposition between *appearance* and *disappearance* with one between *open* and *closed*. In one sense this is a valid hypothesis, since whereas previously Rachid played with his hands and had nothing in mind, now, in operating the garage doors, he was thinking of something that was not present, the Metro carriage. The action no longer eclipsed the thought. Instead it accompanied it. But this formulation is not fully satisfactory because it ignores what was specific to Rachid's games. I shall attempt to define this by comparing his game with three other games: first, the cotton-reel game; second, the games of most children, who would first play with the garage as a garage, then later use it as the Metro; and lastly the game young Dick played with his train in the session reported by Melanie Klein, the founder of child psychoanalysis in Britain (in *The Importance of Symbol Formation in the Development of the Ego* (1930)).

First let us consider Rachid and the story of the cotton reel. Freud tells of his grandson alone in his crib. His mother was out doing the shopping. The child was awake, and Freud observed him. The child played with a cotton reel on the end of a thread. He threw it away from him and hauled it back by pulling on the thread, accompanying his throwing motion with 'gone' and the return of the object with 'there'. This game based on the disappearance and reappearance of a specific object, the cotton reel, was interpreted by the grandfather as a way of coming to terms with the appearance and disappearance of the mother by overcoming in play the sadness of being alone. In the case of Rachid, it looked as though the opening and closing of doors enabled him, too, to make things disappear and reappear (all the things one might put in a garage, for example). However, he did not use the garage in this way. He did not hide anything in it or retrieve anything from it. The opposition inside versus outside played no part. When the door was open the garage was empty, with nothing in it save darkness.

Nor can one accept that the relation between the Metro of Rachid's imagination and the doll's house that he played with symbolizes this game of presence versus absence: unlike the Metro train, the garage did not move and never disappeared from view. It is solely through the game of alternating appearance and disappearance that the cotton reel acquires meaning. Consequently the garage constitutes neither a void that can stand for a container capable of absorbing then restoring things, nor an object that can be made to disappear and reappear. However, a connection between open/closed and presence/absence cannot, it seems to me, be ruled out. But, as we shall see, it is a complex connection.

It has in fact three components. The first is that of the perceptual discontinuity marked by the garage door. When a sliding door is closed, nothing can be seen. We are confronted by a smooth, unbroken surface. When it is open a breach appears. It then becomes an irregularity that catches our attention. This is what René Thom, the mathematical philosopher, terms a 'catastrophe'. And there is no doubt that Rachid has a taste for catastrophes in this sense. Thus we may imagine that his game with the sliding door may be above all a game with the appearance and disappearance of a catastrophe on a regular surface. At this level, the garage door, like the Metro door, allows one to cancel out an irregularity or restore it.

However, the catastrophe represented by the door presents a paradox: if a door is an irregularity on a smooth wall, it is also a frame that makes it possible to isolate within it any object from the surrounding space. It delimits a background: the interior of the room or the vehicle into which it admits entry. And when the two panels of the sliding door are reunited, the rectangle which forms a frame for any object within it disappears. Here, unlike the game with the cotton reel, it is not a material body which appears or disappears, but a frame. And this frame is not merely a thing to be observed but, further, something that lets other things be seen and thought about.

So far so good. But at the same time, when a Metro train closes its doors it is preparing to disappear, for, as the official slogan has it: 'The train cannot leave until all doors are closed,' and the closing of the doors heralds the departure of the train. So there is a connection between the closing of the doors and the disappearance of the train. But when we close the doors of a garage, the garage does not disappear. We may conclude that Rachid enjoyed playing on this difference, and so persuading himself that not all doors that close indicate an immediate disappearance.

When he activated the sliding door, Rachid brought into play a whole gamut of meanings. We are far from the finger motions that in themselves eclipsed any representation. Yet this new game did not rely directly on any anthropomorphic representation. This no doubt is the reason why I was not fully convinced that he had found an equivalent to the cotton reel.

Nor was I convinced that he was playing Metro trains. If I picture to myself the way almost any other child would play this game, it seems to me that the differences are numerous. First, another child would not resort to a house as an accessory, quite simply because a house such as that chosen by Rachid does not move. To make a train, another child would take some building blocks or pieces of Lego and line them up. In other words, he would look for something that could move, appear, and disappear. Rachid's choice, however, was an immobile object in which the sliding door played a central role. The stability of the house was a guarantee that it would not disappear, but at the same time, as we have seen, the closing of the doors signalling the departure of the train indirectly linked this sequence to the idea of absence. It seemed to me that making a game in which opening and closing doors signified the appearance and disappearance of the train indicated a problem in his treatment of presence and absence. It was as if Rachid had no representation of the transition between the moment when the train was at the station and the moment when it had disappeared. In the game of the cotton reel, the fact that it gradually disappeared from the child's field of vision seemed to me important as a perceptual support for the psychic permanence of something that was out of sight: things that do not disappear suddenly have more chance of remaining whole somewhere in the world than those that disappear or appear all at once. When a boy moves a row of blocks to play at trains departing and arriving, his movements implicitly enable him to see all the intermediate stages between outright presence and total absence: he sees everything from the moment he first thinks he can hear something in the depths of the tunnel, through the moment he sees the front of the train emerging, to the point where the whole train finally stops in front of him. These are the signs that, for anyone who uses public transport, mark the stages of the appearance and disappearance of a Metro train at a platform, and the everyday situations that reinforce our feeling that things are not at constant risk of inexplicably appearing and disappearing.

So much for the matter of the absence of movement. There is also the dimension of the train as container: it seems to me that most children would try to put little people into the thing representing the Metro, or to take them out. But the train that Rachid plays with is one that lacks any depth. He puts nothing inside it and takes nothing out, for, in spite of the range of representations evidenced in his game, he remains firmly focused on the manipulation of the door itself. He concentrates on the fact that the garage door operates in the same way as the Metro door, that its sliding action permits it to vanish like that of a Metro train (or a bus), and that this distinguishes it from hinged doors, which move differently through space. These similarities, linked with the fact that you can participate in making them slide, embrace all that forms the essence of the garage door as well as all that forms the essence of the Metro door for Rachid: the one is superimposed upon the other. The result is the obliteration of the peculiarities of both the Metro door and the garage door: the object that Rachid was playing with detached itself from the garage without, however, becoming a Metro door. And there it was suspended in a void, as in a Magritte painting. In one sense, what Rachid seemed to like was as much the action of opening and shutting itself as the fact that it allowed him to act upon the world. This meant that the house was functionally reduced to the status of a sliding frame for the door.

As I watched him, the notion that the faculty of abstraction might be the product of patient assimilation of various concrete situations seemed false, at least in the case of Rachid. He did not move from play to purposeful activity, from the varied to the particular, while stepping back from the specific. He possessed an immediate primitive geometrical sense by which he apprehended the world in fixed and abstract fragments. Perhaps this was linked to an enjoyment of movement and to sensation-based pleasure.

Whether or not this was true, in the case of Rachid the capacity for rigorous logic that enables one to classify objects by their visible features (colour, size, shape) seemed to be more developed than the acquisition of that other logic that invites one to classify objects according to their use in daily life (e.g. grouping boots, a hat, and an oilskin coat together, or a plate, a glass, a knife, and a fork). Rachid's abstract logic prevailed over his feeling for the logic of everyday life. It even seemed as if his abstract logic affected not only his way of constructing the object perceived, but also the form of the object of his affection. One might be forgiven for thinking that the episode of the Metro door is, in essence, merely a geometrical version of the magical way of thinking that leads a child to play with a symbol as if the symbol could actually affect the thing represented by the symbol. In his game with the door of the miniature garage, Rachid can see only its sliding action.

At this point I would like to move on to the question of the undeniable resemblance between Rachid's game and that of young Dick with his two trains, as observed by Melanie Klein.

In that instance, Melanie Klein was confronted by an autistic child. At the moment in the treatment that she describes, the child had progressed beyond the stage of complete self-absorption, which constitutes the primary phase of autism. He seemed to be interested exclusively in trains and openings.

In the session described, there are two toy trains on the floor, one large, one small, and Melanie Klein suddenly points to the big one, and says 'Daddy-train', immediately contrasting it with the smaller train, saying 'Dick-train'. To the surprise of the psychoanalyst, the boy then takes the small train to the window. Melanie Klein comments on this, saying, 'The station is Mummy;

Dick is going into Mummy.' At once the child displays extreme anguish and runs to take refuge in the dark of the double doorway separating the consulting room from the waiting-room. 'Dick is inside dark Mummy,' Melanie Klein then observed. At this point the child calls for his nurse.

This passage has been the subject of much comment, notably by Lacan, who endeavoured to identify what made Melanie Klein's intervention effective. In an autistic child such as Dick, representation is so rare and tenuous that one might suppose that her intervention gave him a grasp of symbolic content that he had totally lacked. By her own admission, nothing in the material of the session gives her grounds to infer what she proposes. It was a purely inductive construction. How, then, does it happen that the child, usually self-absorbed and apathetic, begins to speak and act? Should we postulate a hereditary unconscious that holds memories of things never experienced? We have no way of knowing if the idea that Melanie Klein was referring to had already figured in the child's representations or if it was something she had suggested to him. Neither Lacan nor any other commentator has settled this question.

I shall not attempt to resolve it. To my mind, the real problem lies elsewhere. If Melanie Klein's hypothesis was accurate, this was not because it affected any aspect of the child's representations. In my view, the accuracy of her statements owes more to the fact that she set up a conflict in the child's mind and this conflict compelled him to go further. This needs explaining: Dick knows what a train is; he also knows what he and his father are. He also knows the terms by which they are known and he is able to use language for these purposes. He therefore knows that he cannot take literally what Melanie Klein says when she calls one of the trains 'Dick-train' and the other 'Daddy-train'. Literally, Daddy-train is a train and is not Daddy, and Dick-train is a train, not Dick. Yet the difference in size between the two trains mirrors the difference in size and situation between Dick and his father. To my way of thinking, the thing that 'worked' was the complex system induced by the expressions 'Dick-train' and 'Daddy-train'. These introduced a conflict. Something was being said to Dick that compelled him to modify his use of language, since he understood what Melanie Klein 'meant'. He was therefore compelled to admit that the words 'Dick' and 'Daddy' served here to describe objects, not to identify them. It is not merely the content that operates here, but the fact that in Melanie Klein's expressions 'Dick' and 'Daddy' indicate relative size rather than people. Dick knows that the train he is being shown is neither his father nor himself, but he also observes that the two trains resemble each other and are distinguished by their size, just as he himself resembles his father, from whom he is distinguished by size.

Comparison with the case of Dick helps us to clarify certain aspects of Rachid's behaviour. First, Dick and Rachid have several tastes in common, such as trains, but also openings and orifices—not specifically human (windows and doors)—which an analyst may nevertheless see as representing human orifices. The fact remains, however, that the resemblance is only partial, as we saw a moment ago in the comparison with Freud's grandson and the cotton reel. Dick's game seemed to me both more and less elaborate than Rachid's. More elaborate in its structure, in the fact that Dick moves one of the trains (the shorter of the two) and brings it into contact with the wall in which there is a window, allowing Melanie Klein to say, 'The station is Mummy; Dick is going into Mummy.' Rachid, however, chose as a signal for the Metro something that did not move, and he did not attempt to move it. Dick's game, on the other hand, seemed to me less elaborate in that he did not utter a single word to accompany it, unlike Rachid, who spontaneously said 'Metro'. Above and beyond the fact that one spoke and the other did not, Rachid's choice of word demonstrated that he was able to introduce some absent component, something he was thinking of, into his game. He was functioning on several levels; his movements were not mechanical—they had meaning in his own eyes and were connected with his memory of the Metro.

I would now like to contrast the foregoing with a later episode in Rachid's symbolic development. In the second month of treatment, Rachid took two teddy bears, Mr Bear and Mrs Bear, and suddenly stood them back to back, saying: 'About turn!' This surprised me, but I learned from his mother, who was still present during that session, that Rachid was referring to a television programme in which two people were brought together to collaborate in solving problems posed by the presenters. To complicate matters, the partners were placed back to back. This scene arranged by Rachid reminded me of his mother's avoidance of eye-contact. But the thing that stayed in my mind was the originality of his mode of representation.

The presence of two bears impelled Rachid to place them in a mutual relationship. Unlike the cat-puppet episode, this time the toys were real figurative resources for him. But how was one to understand the train of thought that led him to use the television programme? What route had he followed? Why this complicated procedure? To represent the relations between the couple, another child would probably have mimed directly a scene in which the two bears fought or embraced. We cannot claim that Rachid placed the bears back to back because he had difficulty in finding a gesture that would have made them kiss or fight. One sees plenty of kissing and fight scenes on television. Choosing to place them back to back and remembering 'About turn!' was a way of avoiding placing them face to face. With any other child, I think I would have left it at that, but not with Rachid. It seemed to me that this back-to-back position was also a stable basis on which he could build a story with movement in it, like the departure of the Metro train, represented earlier by the closed doors. A still picture could refer to the totality of a movement, to a sequence. The fixed vision of the two protagonists back to back represented the totality of their story as acted out before the cameras.

This taste for fixed details as a reminder of a much larger sequence of events struck me again when Rachid told me something of his regular visits to the doctor who monitored him once a month at the clinic. To refer to these visits, Rachid said only 'Press 3' as he was seen by the doctor on the third floor and therefore had to press the button marked 3, not 2, in the lift, as he did when he came to see me. We can hardly attribute this manner of speaking to a tendency to simplify when speaking, since Rachid was perfectly capable of pronouncing the doctor's name: 'Doctor A'. Here again a minute fragment of a story—a detail that recalled Rachid's taste for 'catastrophes'—stood for the totality of a memory. It invoked a relationship between himself and this doctor and everything that might be associated with this at the emotional level. Should we also believe that the confined space of the lift constituted a kind of container and biased the choice of a gesture that stood for the whole sequence of evocative events? It is possible.

When Things Change

When we think back over the history of a relationship, even when we have taken notes every day, it is difficult to identify the critical points, those where one is sure that something has crystallized. And when we do identify them, we tell ourselves that they only appear as such because they have been preceded by long periods of fermentation. When I reflect on the sessions with Rachid, however, I can recall several striking moments which, when placed in perspective, resemble one another. Many of them are the product of chance occurrences that suddenly made it possible to enrich one of Rachid's repetitive actions without removing it from the position he had allocated to it in the organization of his rituals.

First there was the door. To reach one of the offices in which our sessions took place it was necessary to pass through a swing door. This door took its place in the series headed 'doors', but with one specific property that distinguished it from the sliding doors of public transport, and from traditional doors that do not swing both ways. Each time we passed through it Rachid would stop and display great interest. He would set it swinging to see how it worked. Since this game had an annoying tendency to go on indefinitely and I wished to reach our room before the end of the session, I would say, 'Just once more, all right?' But all of a sudden I realized I was in front of one of the swinging halves, swaying gently from right to left and left to right, my body replicating the movement of the door, while Rachid observed me, until the door and I stopped moving. He had a rather satisfied air, having shared something with me on his territory, the territory of doors, and having seen that his interest in things of this kind could mean something to me as well, which struck me as rather different from having *a meaning*. And indeed, in replicating by my swaying motion the action of the door, it was not my intention to provide an interpretation that would lend one particular meaning to his interest; I was simply letting him know that I had understood that for him the movement of a door was something that merited interest. And that the swaying motion might be—in addition to the movement of a door—that of a tree or of a couple dancing, or of an adult playing at imitating a door. In short, I was demonstrating to him my sensitivity to the fact that even a movement cannot be reduced to the visible things that move—it could also refer to something other than itself. This in turn evokes the idea that it is possible to act like a door without becoming a door. Similar yet dissimilar. In this light, my movement could have an interpretative or symbolic value: it could show Rachid that I did not hold the view, any more than he did, that, when the attention of two people was focused on the same object, that object could not be reduced to the sum of its parts, even if no words were exchanged. All the same, replicating the movement of the door swinging in time with Rachid's push is not the same as formulating an interpretation. It was more a matter of extending the value of a detail, as if my body served as a clue and made it possible suddenly to bring into play a range of malleable meanings.

Other episodes no doubt contributed to the gradual 'unblocking' of Rachid's rituals. Playing with the lights was one of these. One day Rachid turned off the light. I tried to put into words the anxiety that came over him and that I could discern in him, as well as in his mother who was also present. I said simply: 'It's dark; here comes the wolf.' He seemed to enjoy the situation. He left the light off for a moment, then turned it on again and moved on to something else. But on another occasion, when he went back to counting the felt-tip pens, I deflected his 'one, two, three' into the counting rhyme 'One, two, three, off we go to the wood'. At that point he darted towards the switch and turned out the light. Supposing that he was confusing this with 'Let us stroll in the wood while the wolf is away', I went on with the line about the wolf. This time he seemed more reassured. I drew his attention to the window. I described what I saw outside: one or two people walking past and a car passing, as darkness fell. The combination of light, the theme of the wolf, and the spectacle we watched together through the window provided a positive enrichment for his rituals to come.

It is also possible that the act of looking out of a window in this way absolved Rachid from a cognitive task that he found difficult: following the direction of my gaze in order to identify what it was that held my attention. We know, of course, that being able to direct one's eyes towards something seen by someone else, so as to look at the same object, is a necessary prerequisite for dialogue. In order to communicate, we must be able to turn our minds towards the same things, direct our eyes towards the same signs at the same time. This requires the ability to follow the other person's line of sight to its object, by interpreting the position of the head and eyes. This was a calculation that Rachid was unable to achieve. But in this case the darkness obviated the need to do so: the window immediately provided the place to which we should turn our eyes. And it was obvious that his gaze and mine would converge at any luminous, moving point in the darkened street.

When the light came on again, Rachid saw himself in the black glass that served as a mirror. He immediately started jumping about and invited me to do the same. I said to myself that his request that I should jump about like him was the motor counterpart of our harmonized vision.

On another occasion, the darkness was the starting point for an exchange between him and his mother that was infinitely more elaborate. When I hummed 'One, two, three, off we go to the wood', he came in with 'wolf' and I went on as before: 'let us stroll in the wood'. He then put away our drawings and went to switch off the light, enjoining me to go to sleep with a firm 'Night night!' I pretended to go to sleep, lying down on the bed in my office and imitating his little brother, asking Rachid for the feeding bottle. He refused to give it to me. I replied that in that case I would ask Mummy for it. He proceeded to address his mother (who was still there), with the words, 'No bottle, Mummy', signalling unambiguously that he forbade his mother to give me the bottle that I intended to ask her for.

At the end of this session, no sooner had he left my office than he turned back to me—while his mother was further along the corridor—saying, 'Monsieur Laurent, cagoule?' to let me know that he had lost his rain-hood and that he would like to know if I had found it. I searched for it with him in my office, but in vain. There was no sign of it in the waiting-room either. Slightly downcast, he turned up the hood of his parka and said, 'Cagoule'. He had clearly decided that the parka hood should replace the missing one.

The Whistling Bottle

As a last example of the way Rachid progressed in unpredictable and sudden spurts, here is a game we devised around a stoneware bottle. In an office that I used for one of our three weekly sessions there was a stoneware bottle that Rachid liked. One day he took hold of it and began handling it so roughly that I became slightly anxious and said to him, 'Here, watch this.' I took the bottle from him and blew into the opening to make it whistle. It sounded rather like a foghorn announcing a ship's departure, and this amused Rachid. He took it back and blew into it. The bottle sounded its note.

The bottle played no part in our next session. We looked at a school photograph and I pointed out Rachid. Then in our toybox we came upon a baby doll that did not belong there. I placed the intruder outside the office, behind the door, saying, 'Off you go, baby. You don't belong here.'

The next day Rachid did not come to his session, as sometimes happened. But this made me wonder what he might have made of my expulsion of the baby.

During the session after that we were back in the office where the stone bottle was kept. He began by running through his usual routine on the drawing-board: logos of television stations and Metro lines (M6, FR3, A2 or M12). For M6, as usual, he first wrote the M, beginning at the bottom right, then wrote the 6. For each digit he would usually take a new coloured pencil, placing the figures in a line that stretched across a sheet of paper from one side to the other. But this time he duplicated each sign, repeating it in a different colour (whereas he would usually move from 6 to 7 and so on in regular progression). Furthermore, he commented on what he was writing, in a low murmur in which I thought I heard something like 'wrong mummy', as if he were dictating something to his mother and pointing out her mistakes. What is more, he did not finish his row of symbols, which was unusual.

Then he remembered a recent visit to his consulting specialist, Dr A, changed the subject again, drew some circles in a row, reminiscent of the tenor of our first sessions and of the Metro line maps shown above Metro station entrances. Suddenly the stone bottle found its way into his field of interest and his game. He picked up all the coloured pencils and slipped them one by one into the bottle. He pretended to whistle into it, then sat down on a chair, turned to face the wall, lowered his head and hid his face behind the chair back. Finally he turned again to face me and said he was ill, indicating various orifices one after the other: a nostril, an ear, his mouth, then his 'poo' (his 'poo' hurt; 'doing poo' hurt; his anus hurt). This pain signalled a recognition of his body as having an internal dimension. It had something to do with an empty bottle, which, being empty, could at the same time sound hollow and be filled with pencils.

Once again a link was established between an unusual and circumscribed perception, an inversion of values (the empty bottle makes a sound, while a full one does not), and a fragment of our story that no doubt linked up in a distant way with the episodes of the intrusive baby, the school photograph, his absence, and the visit to Dr A.

It is difficult, of course, to locate precisely the shared features of these key moments, but I was struck by two things. In all cases, the change occurred following the appearance of some minimal sensation, but also thanks to a kind of suspension, some interruption of ritualized motions. In the episode of the darkness, there was the gesture of switching off the light, fear of the wolf in the counting rhyme, the fact of standing beside me to look at luminous objects moving outside. Then there was the matter of his saying 'Night night!' and my performing the action of his little brother going to sleep on the bed. In the episode of the door there were also several changes involving some detail that he singled out. Here it was a door that he liked, but a door of a different type from that of a Metro train. And in this case again I varied the object, simulating the movement by beginning to sway back and forth.

These various changes interrupted the smooth progress of the ritual which, for Rachid, consisted in giving his usual push to the door. He was now obliged to stand idly by, since in order to watch my movements he had to abandon his own movement and think. In the episode of the bottle, the blowing, the movement of the mouth, was the reverse of drinking from a baby's bottle. Instead of sucking, it was necessary to blow. What is more, this action only worked with an empty bottle. And this implied a kind of inversion, since an empty bottle or a baby's bottle with nothing in it is not usually of interest. But this bottle had to be empty in order to produce a sound. By using the bottle as a whistle, Rachid was removing it from its utilitarian function. It no longer suggested only the act of drinking, of sucking, or of pouring. Everything that followed, the crayons, the movements of Rachid who had a sore nose, a sore mouth, and a 'sore poo', demonstrated clearly that as soon as the bottle became something that could not be absorbed into any single ritual, it became the device, the focal point around which a new theme could crystallize, constituting an internal capacity that could be seen in relation to that of the body.

The point in common in these different moments of change seemed to me to rest on a shift in the nature of his act in relation to the process of representation. At first it was rather as if the sudden release effected by the action caused a short circuit that suspended all thought. At the moments we have described the action invariably remained the anchor point of symbolic meaning, but its value was variable. The action accompanied the symbolic value. This was possible because on every occasion the movement was partly suspended or impeded. When we were in the dark, we stopped moving to watch something (and Rachid began jumping in front of his reflection when the light was turned on again). When we blew into a bottle to produce a sound we stopped drinking in order to do something else. We were obliged to interfere with the utilitarian action of sucking. When we watched somebody else's movements, we accepted that we ourselves would not move, and at the same time we inwardly participated in this movement while outwardly remaining still (Rachid did not sway with the door, but as he observed my movements he slightly accompanied them, and if he actually chose not to move, this no doubt was because he was the one who originally set the door in motion).

Each time the trigger is provided by the inception of an opposing movement, or of two movements. A conflict then arises and Rachid ceases one movement or the other. He pauses in acting out a ritual motion. Hence the fact that he regards the bottle as a container. Linked to these thoughts there may be a feeling that draws in the whole of the body rather than just a single part of it. Awareness of darkness involves the whole body (and the feeling of being in the dark is not located in any particular part of the body). In similar fashion, my imitation of the movement of the door involves my whole body and, in a sense, all of Rachid's body as he observes my movements. The emergence of a feeling that has no definite source must also be related to this broadening of meaning. In any event, Rachid is compelled to abandon his strategy of fragmentation and enumeration.

The paradox, of course, is that while things change they remain partially as they were. For example, after some time Rachid himself drew his family: his father, mother, and brother as characters. But when he had finished, he needed to give each one a number: he himself was number twenty-two, his father twenty-one, his brother twenty, and his mother sixty-eight. This gave me food for thought. Was it a way of telling me that he would not change completely? That he was drawing human beings? Was it a way of establishing the position of each: the menfolk—his brother, father, and himself in sequence as twenty, twenty-one, and twenty-two—and his mother alone and remote, like the number sixty-eight in relation to the three others? I do not know.

Sexual Differentiation and Language

I will now describe a series of several sessions during which it seemed to me that some essential points were clarified. We were about eight months into the treatment. Rachid's mother, seeing her son's linguistic progress, wanted to reduce the number of weekly sessions from three to two. I was opposed to this and let her know my view. To decide the issue, I suggested that she seek a consultation with Dr A, which she did. This consultation was recorded on video. When I viewed the recording, Rachid appeared very different to me.

During my next session with him, he spoke straightaway of his visit to Dr A. Everything went as usual. He drew a car, as he sometimes did at this stage; but a car seen from behind, with its outline rounded at the top and including a horizontal rectangle (the rear window) in the upper part, all standing on two circles (the two wheels). He then asked for a pair of scissors to cut round the outline, again taking up a game we had played earlier. (I had even drawn and cut out some figures for use as puppets—to no good purpose, in spite of all my pedagogical zeal.) This time, however, the use of the scissors seemed to galvanize him. He drew a snail and began cutting it out. But as curves are difficult to cut with scissors, he made a mess of it. Then, using our modelling clay, he fashioned a birthday cake for me and handed it to me, saying 'Happy birthday, Monsieur Laurent,' in a nicely pitched tone. He cut it up with a doll's table knife and started chewing his piece. I had difficulty in persuading him to spit it out.

At our next session, the video room in which his previous visit to Dr A had been recorded was vacant. As I had always wanted to observe Rachid and myself at work, I seized the opportunity. Rachid was very quick to point out that this room belonged to Dr A. I played along with him. When he asked for some toy cars to play with, I said that I had none, and that he could have some when he visited Dr A. Clearly the room as a whole and the movements of the camera in particular were to Rachid a kind of material sign of the gaze of the absent Dr A.

This session was particularly fruitful. He produced a number of quite novel images in a manner very much his own; first a lion formed from two rows of vertical lines, one representing its mane, the other its teeth. Then a kind of fish with long paws, which greatly intrigued me. As Rachid did not respond to my requests for clarification on this subject, I said, 'I think Rachid is like a daddy who knows and Monsieur Laurent is like a baby who doesn't know.' This elicited a reply. His drawing represented a shrimp with long thin legs, or possibly antennae. As soon as he had provided this explanation, it became apparent that his drawing had in fact captured something of the spider-like quality of shrimps in a tidal pool at low water. He proceeded to draw a man with a moustache, a car at a red traffic light, and two large flowers, one 'that stings' and one 'that doesn't'. (When this subject came up again later, during a session in which his mother was present, she told me that he was thinking of palms like those he might have seen in his homeland while on holiday.) Lastly there was a curiously aligned boat: the hull was vertical and the sail and keel lay horizontal. When I indicated that our session was over, he resisted and wanted to go on drawing. He drew a door. Again I offered my interpretation: 'That will be something to close, to finish for today.' At this he acquiesced and helped me to tidy up.

Clearly the essential point here was the material weight of the various individuals who existed but were not present. First there was Dr A: the room we were using on this occasion was the one where he met Rachid. There was also the video camera, which marked the presence of a spectator. Given Rachid's interest in television, perhaps he had a vague feeling that those who are filmed are watched by people who cannot be seen. For my part, I sensed clearly that my awareness of a potential audience exerted a certain influence on the way I voiced my interpretations, which were less specific than usual. Moreover, this setting seemed to offer a sort of background or Gestalt, in which Rachid could mark the difference between his relations with Dr A and his relations with me. He certainly did things that signified the absence of Dr A, and I showed that I understood without attempting to compensate for his absence, as if to say, 'I can think of A, whom I also know, and I can tolerate the fact that you have seen him without my being present.' (I had been present only when I was introduced to Rachid and his family.) For the rest, throughout our session Rachid played with me as if everything we did were a repetition of the consultation with Dr A, as if I were A and he were Rachid-with-Dr-A.

Our next session was back in the office with the stoneware bottle. Rachid first asked me to write down the words he dictated—something he had not done for a long time. Among other requests was one to 'draw' some water (by which he meant that I should write the word 'water'). When I took a blue crayon and drew a wave, pretending not to understand, he protested and scratched out my drawing, which he described as 'scribbing'. Then on another sheet he asked me to write the word 'water'. As soon as I had written it he tried to rub it out. I then took a blue felt-tip and ran it over the word, which disappeared under it. He wrote some series of letters, then the words 'water' and 'fire'. No sooner had he written this last word than he drew a circle round it and said it was in Mummy's tummy. Above the circle containing the word 'fire' he drew two eyes and a mouth, and below it two legs.

He then asked me to write a series of words: pasta, ketchup, yoghurt, fruit, spectacles. I drew a pair of glasses next to the word I had just written. He asked me to draw a butterfly beside the expression 'butterfly pasta' and allowed me to draw a bottle of ketchup beside the word 'ketchup'. A little while later he left the drawing-board and went over to a toy dinner set in another corner of the room. He took out a plate and some knives and forks. I was struck by the fact that the bottle from which he pretended he was pouring ketchup (an imitation made of green-painted wood, actually more like a wine bottle) could not serve as a bottle of orange juice in the game, in spite of my request. I was even more surprised when I asked him for a piece of chocolate and he could only offer me a puppet, because its head was the colour of dark chocolate. He did not offer, for example, a flat square of yellow wood, which might have confronted me less directly with my cannibal nature. Then he again began asking me to write down lists of words. The end of our session was approaching and I could sense that this bothered him. Furthermore, as this was the holiday period, he would not be returning to school after the session. I said that he was asking me to write these words because he was unhappy that the session was ending and because his teacher would not be there. He gave the basket of crayons a kick, confirming for me that my interpretation was in line with what he might be feeling, even a little too close to the mark considering the circumstances.

During our next session he drew a man's head, then another circle beneath it, and in this lower circle something that might have represented breasts. I said that it was a fat lady. He responded by drawing a sort of lightning flash originating in her stomach, and beside it he wrote the word 'water'. I decided to turn a blind eye to his attempt to provide the fat lady with attributes of the opposite sex, and said simply, 'I see, she's doing a wee.' He then took a fresh sheet of paper and on one side of it drew a girl, saying, 'This is a girl,' and on the other a boy, of whom he said, 'This is a boy.' Then, as if somewhat alarmed by his own daring, he returned to his accustomed rituals and marked a series of dashes and dots, then a letter, changing colour methodically each time. In the following session he seemed to speak much more.

The salient element in these sessions is the sequence between the allusions to Dr A's absence and the activation of speech, with the differentiation of the sexes in between. It was as if Rachid had suddenly effected in foreshortened form a recapitulation of the key moments in the construction of symbolic system, as commonly described. If I try in retrospect to identify a possible catalyst, I naturally think of the material role of the video room which provided a base from which to evoke the memory of Dr A and note his absence. I also think that the presence of the video camera had an effect upon me. It impelled me to spell out more fully what I sensed, as if I had wished to clarify matters for Rachid, but also for any future viewer.

Where Does this Leave Us?

We have now completed a year of treatment. What has changed? First and foremost, Rachid has *unlearned* much. In his use of numbers he is beginning to say anything that comes into his head. He behaves like a child who makes things up. As for the letters of the alphabet, here too he sometimes makes mistakes, especially in spelling his brother's name, which no doubt is significant. Is he unlearning or is he uninterested? It is difficult to say. Whichever is the case, his more relaxed attitude can also be seen in the humour with which he subverts his own mental categories (during a game of cards he once asked me to play a twelve of diamonds and a fifteen of spades). It sometimes happens now that Rachid will make some slip of the tongue, addressing me as 'daddy' then correcting himself with 'Monsieur Laurent'. In the same vein, and unlike the episode of the ketchup bottle which could not serve as an orange-juice bottle, he now sometimes uses felt-tip pens as aeroplanes, having first used them as felt-tips, so that together we can simulate the flight of a squadron. Furthermore, when he wanted me to pinch off a piece from a firm ball of play-dough, he recently said to me quite simply, 'Open it, Monsieur Laurent'. This was evidence of spontaneous recourse to metaphor, just as one may observe in small children when their desire to communicate is not yet backed by an adequate stock of vocabulary.

Many things have evolved thanks to a change in the value of gestures. For Rachid, gestures were primarily a means of relieving tension. In his dealings with me he has developed the capacity to postpone the complete execution of his gestures without forgetting their meaning. Once he learned to use a bottle to pretend to drink and at the same time to imitate the sound of a departing boat he could establish a connection between two gestures. As they were connected by the bottle, each of these gestures could in a sense stand for the other. But when one gesture stands for another it takes its place in a network of associations and references. In parallel with his acquisition of these capacities, new constructions arose. For instance, just before the Christmas holidays, on returning from an appointment at the hospital to have his hearing checked and not finding me at once in the waiting-room, he gave me to understand that he thought I had also gone to the hospital. Then, during the same session, he imagined me asleep at home, then waking up and drinking some Nesquik for breakfast. In other words, he could now imagine what my life was like when I was not with him, even if his idea of my life closely paralleled his own activities.

At the same time, of course, he retained certain of his idiosyncrasies. His interest in numbers waxed and waned, but remained with him. He still preferred drawing doors and windows, rather than people with big heads. Moreover, when he did draw human figures, he often left them armless, which I still find puzzling. And he seemed to show no real interest in the product of his work except when he was drawing square suns. When he produced drawings of round suns and human figures like those drawn by all other children of his age, he did not look at them. They were merely the product of a series of hand motions. Could the use of a door or a window instead of a man with a big head be simply one individual's way of building a system of symbols?

Today Rachid expresses himself with ease. He can communicate with adults and with his peers alike. But certain aspects of his thought processes, such as his representation of time, are still awkward. Rachid very quickly grasped the recurrent sequence of the days of the week. He was able to name them and register the days of our next meeting from one session to the next. But until very recently his grasp of the notion of yesterday and tomorrow remained uncertain. It is possible that the days of the week provided him with a stable framework within which time may be contemplated, whereas terms such as yesterday and tomorrow, which presuppose some foresight or retrospection with regard to the moment of speech, were difficult for him to master. The days of the week resemble a series of boxes which follow one another in ritual fashion. But yesterday and tomorrow are a way of picturing to oneself what has already happened or what is going to happen independently of ritual motions. And it is this that he found difficult.

I hope that Rachid's taste for change will stay with him, just as I retain a memory of a shared pleasure in making use of the unexpected: a swing door, a whistling bottle. Like the foghorn of a departing ship.

5

Benjamin:
Reality and Fiction

I sometimes wonder whether children's tendencies to create fantasies in which fiction and reality are disturbingly mingled is not encouraged by the fact that words are only indistinct shapes in their minds and they cannot depend upon them to fend off ideas that seem threatening. They cannot express themselves clearly, and are trapped in a state of mental uncertainty among signifiers with fuzzy outlines.

The case history which follows is that of a boy who, when I met him, could speak, but not very well, could not read, and often gave me the impression that he could not clearly distinguish between his imaginary world and the real world. It occurred to me that this confusion had something to do with his backwardness in language. In working with him I therefore alternated analytical listening and more specifically pedagogical work.

A Silent Picnic

Benjamin was a Moroccan boy of 7, thin, taciturn, and not very lively. Yet considerable hopes had been vested in him by his family, where he was the youngest boy. Since his problems seemed to be of a varied nature—he also had hearing difficulties—and since he had already been in the care of a speech therapist, the medical member of our team suggested that the two of us might have a joint session.

On the first visit his mother was with him. When we came into the waiting-room she was going through a piece of poetry with him. We asked if she wished to attend the session and she readily accepted. When we had taken our seats in the office I asked Benjamin if he knew why the four of us were meeting. 'What?' he asked. 'More slowly. I didn't understand!' I then repeated my sentence, trying to ensure that his mother did not speak for him. As he said nothing, I suggested that he might like to draw something, and he did so. When he had finished I asked what he had drawn. 'A man,' he said. 'Has this man got a name?' As he said nothing, I suggested the first name that came into my head: 'Mister Hat'. I wrote this beneath the drawing, pointing out that the man was not wearing a hat. Benjamin immediately drew one. Although he could not really read, and although he may not have heard me

perfectly, he had caught on at once. It seemed as if the association
of the spoken and the written word had made things easier. I then
asked , 'Where is Mister Hat going?' Silence. Remembering that,
during his first consultation with the doctor, Benjamin had drawn
some birds at a 'picnic' (at a zoo where his class had had a picnic),
I said, 'He's going to the zoo.' This time Benjamin heard me and
drew the bars of a cage. 'What kind of animal is in it?' Silence.
I suggested a lion. Benjamin drew one and beneath it I wrote 'lion'.
Then I asked the name of this lion. 'Panther,' he replied. I wrote
'panther' beneath the word 'lion'. Some misunderstanding must
have occurred. No doubt the fact of having written the word for the
animal beneath its cage prevented Benjamin from giving it a
personal name, and perhaps he was giving me the word for another
animal. I pressed on: 'What else is there in this zoo? Are there any
birds?' 'Yes,' said Benjamin, 'some chicks!'

He drew some chicks, under which I wrote 'chicks', observing
that perhaps he really meant little birds. Benjamin went on,
'They're eating bread and fish.' I wrote, 'The birds are eating bread
and fish.' Then, to see how he coped with the written word, I asked
him to point out to me the words 'fish' and 'bread'. He did this,
but picked the wrong word for each. I repeated, 'The birds are
eating bread and fish,' counting out ten syllables on my fingers.
When it was his turn he counted, bending his fingers as he did
so, but instead of enunciating the syllables, he simply counted on
his fingers: 'One, two, three, four, five, six, seven, eight, nine, ten.'
The number at which he stopped corresponded to the number of
syllables in the sentence. Again I was somewhat surprised.

At this point I stopped and showed him the various things he
and I had written. While we looked at the drawing and the written
phrases together, I tried to restart the game: 'If you drew a boat,
Mister Hat could sail somewhere in it.' On hearing the word 'boat',

Benjamin showed sudden animation: 'Morocco! There are lots of uncles there…' And he took my chalk to draw a boat and its anchor, without naming them. Pointing to the anchor, he said to me, 'That's to hook onto rocks or in the sand.' Then he launched into an elaborate tale of a big boat that catches fire. The survivors escape in a small boat. There are bombs, 'des bombes lacry…' (tear-gas bombs). He left this word unfinished. I prompted him, 'lacrymogènes', and when he asked what this was I explained: 'Bombs that sting your eyes and make you cry. Have you ever seen any?' 'Yes, once. In the square. I washed my eyes and afterwards I looked at the footpath and paid attention when I crossed the road. There was a crossroads and I didn't know which way to go…'

His story became muddled again, so I asked him to draw the two roads for me. To my great astonishment, instead of using two parallel lines to represent a road and four intersecting lines for the crossroads, he marked it as a dot from which three arrows diverged. I was intrigued by this scheme, centred on the crossroads, in which Benjamin did not indicate the position of the roads in relation to one another. Instead, he presented his point of view from the crossroads, at which he must choose one of them. The session came to an end. Before leaving, Benjamin's mother stressed the fact that he did not always understand what she said to him, whether in French or Arabic.

I was struck by Benjamin's sudden surge of enthusiasm, inspired by the word 'boat'. I was also convinced that the way his imaginary world encroached on the real was aggravated by his difficulties of hearing and speech. On the one hand, Benjamin needed to speak of the things that haunted him. On the other, as soon as he warmed to them, he became confused.

Perhaps adopting a pedagogical stance at the outset would allow Benjamin a certain distance that would limit this confusion. But only if it did not cause him to put completely aside the thing that worried him. Since I could find no stance that was fully satisfactory, there was nothing I could do but wait and listen.

The Uses of Board Games

In our second session we played the board game known as *petits chevaux*, which resembles ludo. Benjamin found it puzzling. He turned the board this way and that, seeming to be vexed by the columns that intersected in the middle, with figures written in them, only some of which he could read at a time. When one was written the right way up, the next was upside down. He did not understand that a drawing could be oriented to a perspective other than his own, or that a person sitting opposite him might be able to read something that for him was upside down. He could not fully accept that the game did not conform to the logic of his representation of the intersecting columns. After a while he resigned himself to this, and all four of us played—his mother, the speech therapist, Benjamin, and I. At our urging, Benjamin took charge of things. He called out the numbers on the dice and counted out the squares for all the players as they moved their pieces. But on several occasions, when he should have been moving his horses forwards, he moved them backwards. It is true that his mother also confused the direction of movement and lost count of the squares. Benjamin was embarrassed by her awkwardness and felt obliged to play in her place, though he derived little pleasure from this role.

In later sessions we played this game again. With time he took more interest. He explained how he had 'dummied' one of us.

His mother also seemed to enjoy these sessions and laughed as she thwarted her son's plans. She remained perplexed, however, with regard to the effectiveness of the method. Playing games was all very well, but she wanted him to learn to read. One day she complained that he was a 'little rascal' who refused to do his homework by himself and only wanted to have fun. She had even had to give him a smack to get him to come to the session. In view of her frustration, and fully aware that the smack was partly aimed at us (we also played games instead of working), I felt that I owed her an explanation. What we do here, I said, is not quite like school; we play games because we believe that our games may help Benjamin tell right from left, top from bottom, and all the things that are necessary in order to learn to read. Benjamin, who was present during this conversation, watched us. I then addressed him directly, to say that I was prepared to help him but would wait for him to ask for it. Immediately, as if on the defensive, Benjamin replied that when he grew up he would be able to read. This reply, which was a way of telling me that he did not need my help to learn to read—since reading developed naturally with age, like learning to walk—also made reading seem a grown-up skill, coveted and disturbing. 'You know,' I said to him, 'I think you'll be able to read before you grow up.'

Flights of Imagination

A few sessions later I suggested another parlour game, one based on a naval battle. In great excitement, he told me that he had almost the same game at home but 'it goes boom when you shoot from one ship at another'. We each arranged our fleets. At a given moment, as he was trying to move his ships, my colleague pointed out that the ships did not move. At this Benjamin suddenly launched into a world of fantasy. He asked if there was any treasure in the water, and added that when he grew up he would be able to swim where there was a lot of water. Questions followed concerning the reality of treasure under the sand of the seabed and about the sharks and snakes which, he maintained, lived under the sand. It was difficult to tell if he really meant 'under' the sand, as he often confused *sous* (under) and *sur* (on). Then he took a deep breath, as if to calm down, and said that, according to his father, treasure did not exist.

I sensed that Benjamin's mother felt uncomfortable, faced with this torrent of words. In order to leave him room to indulge his imagination without causing her excessive anxiety, I suggested that this tale of buried treasure and snakes sounded like a dream. He half accepted that it did. At once his mother asked him to give the date of the dream. 'Last week, last holiday,' he replied vaguely. She wanted to learn more about these dreams and about what his father might have told him about treasure. But Benjamin changed the subject. He asked if we could play sea battles again. Then, as the snakes reminded him of animals seen in cartoons, he tried to draw them. On one sheet he drew something that resembled the pincers of a crab, a jaw, or mechanical pincers. Between the arms of the pincers he drew a circle, saying that this was 'the eye'. Then he drew another circle beside it: 'That's the food.' This part of his drawing and his way of naming it formed a sort of amalgam, a kind of condensation of food consumed, the orifice through which it is consumed and, no doubt, the anus as well. He started to ask me what I thought of this monstrous orifice, but changed his mind and cancelled the question. I told him that I sometimes had dreams too. He then began telling another story, saying that his father had told him the worst nightmare in the world, featuring devils and Draculas. 'My father,' he said, 'can cast out the devil from a lady by putting God's book on her head. He's even gone to the lady's house in the Metro and done it there.'

This time his mother interrupted. She seemed to be annoyed. Could this be because Benjamin had mentioned his father's power? Or was he close to revealing a family secret? To steer the conversation back towards herself, she began telling me how in her own country she had really seen a woman possessed who had had her demons driven out by a great marabout. This was followed by a death, but from her story I could not understand whether it was the death of this woman or that of the spirit which spoke through her in a male voice. While his mother was telling this story, Benjamin drew the head of the possessed woman, pointing out to me that inside her head was the head of the devil. His mother clearly wondered what we would make of all this. She would have preferred not to have these matters aired in front of her son. I explained to her that it did not concern me whether or not Benjamin was telling the truth. What mattered to me was that he should want to think and talk about something.

Faced with the richness and complexity of the situation, the intertwining of the cultural, the psychological, the scholastic, and the organic (an audiogram also showed that Benjamin's slight deafness was a serious hindrance to him), my colleague and I felt a little out of our depth. Certainly the child needed to be able to assert his mental independence from his mother and think for himself, but this emancipation should not make her feel in any way deprived. Furthermore, while we had to pay attention to Benjamin's hallucinatory fantasies, in the hope of protecting him from his own excesses, too much attention would not be good for him. Part of his excitement could stem from the interest we displayed, but he was also asking us to place limits upon him.

What Do a Volcano and a Kite Have in Common?

The next time, Benjamin was accompanied by his father, who was not eager to take part in the session. We played a game in which one had to pair drawings of familiar objects. Benjamin was very good at it. To help him progress towards the written word, I wrote down the names of the pairs as he found them and dictated them to me. He had difficulty with some simple names such as 'green beans' and 'cherries'.

Then a strange thing happened. Faced with a black boar (where no visual confusion was possible), Benjamin said, 'A hedgehog.' I do not believe that he had really mistaken the one for the other, but rather that he had only one name for all those animals which, on the one hand, have the general appearance of pigs, and, on the other, differ from them by their dark colour and coarse fur.

This error revealed the way in which his search for words functioned, and how it was modelled on recognition of the object. The snout and the bulky shapes formed a generalized profile of 'a pig'. This activated the area of vocabulary that included 'boar' and 'pig'. Then the differences between the animal in question and the prototype, the pig, led to the identification of a particular sub-type, the one that included the boar and the hedgehog. Benjamin suggested 'hedgehog' because this was the only animal of that type that he knew. The words to express any finer distinctions were not in his vocabulary. Benjamin could see the difference in size, but he lacked the word to name an animal that resembled a large hedgehog.

A phenomenon of the same type occurred with a white-dappled fawn. When he saw it, Benjamin said, 'It's a zebra.' He could recognize a quadruped of the family of donkeys, horses, etc. He also noticed a feature of its coat, the contrasting light markings on a dark background, and defined a subclass that included fawns and zebras. But, lacking adequate vocabulary, even though he could see the difference between stripes and spots, he called the spotted animal a zebra. As in the case of the hedgehog, we see first the general definition, then the construction of a characteristic subclass.

In this example, Benjamin had difficulty with words. He confused them and his thinking was imprecise; but sometimes his mental processes seemed to be of a different nature and led to confusion between the real and the imaginary. One day, for example, Benjamin mentioned something he remembered from a holiday. He was on a beach. He was flying a 'volcano', which he kept airborne above his head by running. I listened without fully understanding. However, as he went on with his description I realized that he was speaking of a kite. One might suppose that this was a matter of simple confusion causing him to use one word in place of another, no doubt because of the similarity between the two signifiers *voler* and *volcan* and the fact that three of the same consonants—V, C, L—appeared in *cerf-volant* and *volcan*, although in a different order. But there was more to it than this. What Benjamin called a volcano was to him not merely a misnamed kite. The object that he had in mind became a sort of cross between a kite and a volcano, which reminded him at the same time of incandescent lava hurled skyward and the flight of the piece of fabric on the end of a string above that windswept beach.

Another example that arose was not in the category of personal reminiscences but in that of general knowledge. In a children's magazine we came upon a text explaining that tortoises lay their eggs in the sand. I asked Benjamin what other 'animals' lay eggs. To my surprise he replied, 'Rabbits.' I am quite sure that he knew what a rabbit was, and that he knew very well that rabbits do not lay eggs. What then was the process that led to this reply? It seemed to me that the point of departure was that the tortoise is an animal that one would not expect to lay eggs, and that if tortoises do lay eggs anything might be expected. Finally, the word 'animal', which I had used in my question, if appropriate for tortoises and rabbits, is less so for the category of birds. To Benjamin, a rabbit was an animal but a bird was not. A bird is a bird. Animals should run about on the ground. A fish was probably not an animal either. The word 'rabbit' probably came to his mind because of the association between a tortoise and a rabbit, or rather a hare, in the fable. Or perhaps Benjamin, being a city boy, formed some connection between rabbits on farms and chickens in farmyards...

Whatever the explanation, the way in which his vocabulary was organized posed a basic problem and prevented him from thinking 'bird' when I said 'animal'. To see if it was the word that created the barrier, I rephrased my question, without seeking any correction: 'Who else lays eggs?' To this he replied, 'Cockerels.' The fact that I had retracted the word 'animal' allowed Benjamin to proceed from 'laying' to the lexical field of 'egg-layers', in which the words 'hen' and 'cockerel' are linked. At this point, it is true,

Benjamin confused the two. But he confused them in the way that small children can confuse 'turning on' and 'turning off' lights. Of course, other reasons might always be found for this confusion of the words for cockerels and hens. But these reasons are not mutually exclusive.

Symbolization and the Speech Mechanism

Benjamin's linguistic uncertainty frequently placed him in situations where it was difficult to tell if his unusual responses were the product of his imagination, of failure to understand, or of mistaken choice of words.

Of course, words were not the root of everything. Benjamin's problems with language do not explain all his difficulties. He could sometimes make absolutely clear statements, but this did not necessarily entail a sharper distinction between fiction and reality.

One day, when he was accompanied by his father and the speech therapist was unavoidably absent, the two of us were alone in the office. He began by showing me a 5-franc coin and entrusting it to me, asking me to give it back at the end of our session. I suggested a game of syllable-counting. In mid-game, however, provoked by the word 'horse', Benjamin suddenly launched into another of his flights of fancy: 'In my country there are horses, and a cat.' He followed this thought, wondering if cats and rats made the same amount of noise and which was afraid of the other. As he became confused, unable to say which of them feared the other, I asked him to draw them one after the other. Then I wrote 'cat' and 'rat' under the pictures, and asked, 'What's this cat's name?'

'Marc,' replied Benjamin.

He added that he could write it down and proceeded to do so without error. On this occasion he was able to give a proper name to an animal that he had assigned to a species that he had named; although, of course, Marc is an uncommon name for a cat. He then returned to the matter of the animals in his country, and described them: 'They are in a "thing" for the dead. In a paradise.' No doubt he had heard that the animals that roamed free in his country seemed to be in a real paradise. But death was also lurking in the background. Then he said the word 'bull' and spoke of a big bull that he had approached 'very close' and that was dangerous. He stopped and asked me, 'Do bulls die when their thing gets broken?' (he indicated a horn). I replied that bulls did not die when they lost a horn. He went on, 'Bulls have a bump on their backs with blood in it. All animals have the same bump. So have I.' He pointed to his knee. This was his bump. The session continued in this way, following Benjamin's chain of associations and his questions. 'Which is the strongest animal of all? A big elephant or a little elephant?' I pointed out that big elephants are very strong but little ones are also capable of defending themselves. 'My granny said that once, before we were born, the animals used to talk.'

Several times during this excited burst of speech, Benjamin stopped himself. I saw him trying to catch an invisible speck of dust in the air. He often did this, he told me, but one should not do it too often. 'Did you do it,' he asked, 'when you were little?' The meaning of this action puzzled me. What induced him to catch a half-imagined speck of dust? Hallucinations? Habit? Or could it be a floater in his eye that travelled with his eye movements and troubled him?

A little later, Benjamin spoke of the sky, in which there were large balls of fire with smaller balls inside them. He drew a ball of fire like the sun and put a smaller ball within it, with the earth beneath them. Having finished his drawing, he raised his head and asked, 'Can these balls hear us?' I related this to the absence that day of his mother and my colleague the speech therapist. 'I believe you'd like your mother and the other lady to hear us,' I said. He went on, 'When the balls of fire fall down they "slap-crash-smash" everything and the sea puts the fire out. Do you think they smash everything?' 'No, I don't think they do. They can't fall down,' I replied.

Thus, when he was alone with me, his imagination took wing. When I referred to this indirectly by asking if he would like his mother and the other lady to be present, he replied with a very positive 'yes'. I added that he could, like me, think of them even when they were not there. He conceded this, as if accepting, with reassurance, that I could guarantee their permanence even though they were absent.

Then he resumed his questions: 'Why is the earth so small when outside everything around us is so big?' Or, 'How do babies come out of their mummies' stomachs?' He kept at me until I said that babies come out between their mothers' legs because women are made differently from us. Benjamin followed this with a new twist in his thinking, this time to describe to me the way a baby is fed by 'the thing behind in its mummy's mouth in her tummy'. He went on: 'The baby hears but it can't eat.' And again he sought confirmation from me of his knowledge, in which imaginary theorizing about babies mingled with information culled from magazine photos and films about life within the womb. Our session came to an end. As I saw him to the door I forgot to return his 5-franc coin. He was the one who asked for it back.

A child whose mind is so taken up with the imaginary has neither the time nor the mental space for academic learning. This is why he still could not read. Shortly after this, however, came a session that I believe enabled Benjamin to learn to read properly.

When I went out to meet him, Benjamin was playing a game with his mother. He wanted to bring the game into our session, but I would not let him. I had decided to read with him.

I read aloud, running my finger along the lines. After a while I encouraged him to read with me, but suddenly he stopped and, at a point in the book where a boy is holding a balloon by a string, he expressed his wish to fly. Once again we launched into a sort of reverie provoked by a speech about the search for God and an encounter with him. As he became more and more carried away, his language became less precise and I was not always able to follow. But it seemed that he was telling me of a plan he and his brother had conceived to leap from the roof of a hut in Morocco and fly. Then he asked why some balloons fly and others do not, and how many balloons one would need to fly off into the sky. To return his attention to our reading, I suggested an exercise we had practised before, in which he pointed with his index finger to certain words which I read to him. He hesitated, then raised his second finger skyward in a rude gesture and said to me, 'It's a sin to do like this, eh?' To which I replied, 'With that finger, yes. But not with this one.' I showed him my index finger and suggested he use it to follow the words in the text. Then came a question about the holy book, the Koran: 'That book has magic powers because my father saved a lady who was possessed by demons. Did God make it?' Without giving a direct answer, I said, 'Could it be that you are afraid of reading because you are afraid of reading the holy book, like your father?' He denied this. But I had the impression that I had touched on something. A few sessions later he began reading with real fluency. Of course it is impossible to ascertain the relative value of this interpretation of his anxiety and guilt about acquiring knowledge (reading meant finger-pointing, and this was a sin) and the role of our syllable exercises. All of this, in addition to the pedagogical work we did together, had a positive effect on his development.

Psychoanalysis and Linguistics

While the alternation of a psychoanalytical session with a more pedagogical one helped Benjamin to structure differences and oppositions, and permitted us to address directly the difference between men and women, between fiction and reality, between true and false, this was insufficient to allay Benjamin's anxieties. Some time after the episode of the finger and his beginning to read, I took out a box of toys containing some animals. Benjamin asked, 'Is there any blood inside the hippopotamus?' He did not appear to be joking. 'No,' I said. 'There isn't any blood because these aren't real animals.'

'No,' he replied. 'They're not real because if they were you couldn't put them in that box, or else they'd be so small that they'd be crushed.'

The real and the imaginary were intersecting. Knowing full well that the animals were not real, he feared that the toys contained blood. He did not take the hippopotamus for a real animal but he sought confirmation that his thoughts had not penetrated the plastic figure.

No doubt Benjamin's uncertainty here was not a matter of mere words. Yet, the distance from his questions to an enquiry into the limits of the arbitrariness of signs is not great.

Our work together came to an end two years ago. Benjamin is now proceeding with normal schooling. I see him from time to time. He has grown and seems to pay attention to what is said to him. When he does not understand, he says clearly, 'I didn't hear.'

6

Pierre:
Thinking with
Broken Speech

Writing may frequently offer a second chance in a child's speech development. It makes it possible to keep things at a distance, to objectivize and formulate without haste. At least this was my impression during my intermittent work with a 17-year-old whose symptoms included severe speech difficulties. Gradually, beginning with a game using pictograms, he learned to conceptualize the function of writing and more broadly that of language. In a word, he became a grammarian. Although his speech problems have not gone away, one day he began to write stories that were remarkable in their rigour, in spite of their extremely economical syntax.

Pierre: Elegance and Awkwardness

Physically, Pierre was a very thin adolescent, with fine features. His well-groomed elegance contrasted with his rather vacant gestures and inexpressive face. His lack of eye-contact, slow speech, and often garbled utterances indicated the difficulty he had not only with language but with making contact with others. More often than not, when I spoke to him, he seemed to show no reaction. Lost in his own thoughts, he would remain impassive, his eyes fixed on the ceiling, so that I could not tell if he was somewhere else or if he was looking for the words with which to reply. Given time, he would eventually reply, but his responses were brief, pared down to a few essential words, without articles, prepositions, or auxiliary verbs. His lack of grammar, combined with great difficulties in pronunciation (he pronounced B like P, and V like F) often made it hard to understand him. He knew this, and it made him the more timid. It may also have explained why he was not eager to take the initiative in conversation.

This overall impression needs to be qualified, however. First, Pierre had learned to read and write, even if what he wrote was barely intelligible because of his spelling mistakes. But in spite of his linguistic handicap, he had a certain sharpness of mind which he managed to develop. As we shall see, this enabled him to reflect to some extent on his own use of language. Curiously, he was able to detach himself from the *content* of what he had to say, so as to reflect on the *form* of his message. I therefore based my work with him on this capacity, which stemmed no doubt from an unfailing interest in cultural pursuits. Pierre went to the theatre occasionally and enjoyed it greatly. He was also very fond of stories and often asked me to read one to him.

If he was awkward in activities requiring precise motor control (his writing was clumsy and speech was a great effort), he possessed a degree of skill in other areas. For example, he was able to take part in and enjoy various team sports.

When I first met him, Pierre had been monitored regularly for several years by psychotherapists and educational specialists. Lately there had been general agreement that there was new progress in his development. He was beginning to emerge from his shell and was more ready to make contact with other people. I was invited to become involved in order to exploit this positive psychological development in the field of language.

So when we set to work, Pierre could already write, but it was clear that for him writing was simply a transposition of the spoken word. At the same time, however, he spoke so badly that it was very difficult for him to use what he said as a basis for transcription. All my efforts were therefore directed towards showing him that pencil and paper offered a way of registering his thoughts that was less laborious and more accurate than the spoken word, as long as the written word could be separated from the spoken. To achieve this, I offered him a kind of crash course on writing, the arbitrary nature of signs, the systems of syntax, and communication. I believe that this course helped him to take matters into his own hands and take corrective action.

Writing and Absence

During our first conversation I suggested that Pierre, since he was able to read and write, might think of a word—that is, an idea—then try to find a way to represent it by a sketch on paper. He thought of 'tennis' and drew a rectangle to represent a tennis court. I myself would most likely have drawn a racket and ball. Then I said to him, 'If you had left this drawing on the door of my office, I would have understood you to mean you weren't coming because you were at a match.' I added, 'Now, what would you have done to let me know you had gone home?' In reply he drew a door. The ease with which he picked up the idea told me that he accepted my suggestion regarding the fundamental link between writing and absence, and the need—implicit in a pictogram—to reduce things to essentials. He had clearly grasped the function of writing. He had realized intuitively that it was not a matter of a simple encoding and decoding technique but a special mode of communication that makes it possible to leave signs to convey some idea to a third party (being at a tennis match; going home). The difficulty lies in making the signs precise enough to avoid ambiguity and misunderstanding. Especially as the recipient is not there to give us a chance to rectify any potential misunderstanding.

Of course, this realization was not enough to enable Pierre to master writing. But it lent his efforts some meaning, and I hoped that this would help him redouble his efforts later to improve his capacity for decrypting and transcribing. What mattered to me was to give coherence to the disparate fragments of knowledge that he already possessed, while helping him to see that writing serves *to convey ideas*. It seemed to me that only after this would he be able to accept the idea of breaking words down into syllables, then into phonemes so as to try to transcribe them. In order to accept the notion of breaking one's speech down into little meaningless pieces, mutilating it by cutting it into syllables then phonemes, one must first understand that in French one cannot do anything else if one wishes to set down ideas in black and white. In order to do this, it is necessary to become personally acquainted with the whole history of writing and to trace the process from pictograms to letters.

A large number of writing systems in fact begin with the use of pictograms, that is, signs that stand for concepts. But in order to evolve they must all, including the most ideographic, resort to signs that stand not for *concepts* but for *sounds*. If we can manage to convey this to children without inflicting a writing lesson upon them, they will be able to assimilate the alphabetic principle as a real necessity and not merely an irksome academic exercise.

In general, writing is used to communicate with somebody who is not present. The absence of direct visual or auditory contact means that we can never be sure of being understood. We have none of the nods or blinks of assent or uncertainty, none of the little murmurs of 'uh-huh' that tell us that verbal communication has been established. Nor have we any possibility of accompanying our speech by gestures or motioning towards things. In speech we can always exclaim 'ashtray!' and hope that our hearer will snatch an ashtray from a neighbouring table. But in writing, as no comparable situation can be shared, the word 'ashtray' alone does not correspond to any particular ashtray. Hence the banal but essential fact: the run-of-the-mill written sign does not designate an object; instead it refers to a general concept.

Writing necessarily imposes abstraction. The whole history of writing illustrates this. It is a direct consequence of the black hole that separates the writer from the reader. The pictogram for 'fish', for example, does not refer to any specific fish but to the concept, the idea of fish, an aquatic creature with scales, fins, and gills. And any message aimed at an absent reader, since it will be interpreted at some other place and time, demands that its author make a determined effort to stand back from the particular situation in which it was composed. This is an essential point which must be made clear to children: 'If when you write "fish" you don't want me to think of the fish in my aquarium when you mean the fish in the goldfish bowl in your room, the sign meaning "fish" must be limited to the general idea of fish. And if you are determined to indicate to me the fish in your goldfish bowl, we must agree on an arbitrary sign to point out that you mean that one in particular.'

When children feel that a pictogram means an idea, they can then pinpoint the difference between the pictogram and the drawing. A drawing always corresponds to a particular object. A pictogram does not. From this moment on, children are ready to grasp the difference between the three kinds of auditory or written sign that they may encounter: signs that refer to an *idea*, such as 'fish', which can immediately become a pictogram; signs that designate a single *individual*—proper names such as Pierre, Jules, or Marseilles—that require a pictogram-puzzle to represent the sound; and finally those that establish a *relation* between two other signs, functional or grammatical words such as 'of', 'from', or 'in': 'the fish *in* my goldfish bowl'. In rudimentary pictograms these latter signs are not shown. It is the relative position of the other pictograms that enables the reader to restore them. A pictogram of a fish next to one of a goldfish bowl denotes something like 'the fish from the goldfish bowl', or 'a fish from a goldfish bowl', or 'the fish in the goldfish bowl'. The reader supplies these according to the context. It is only when we wish to be more precise that we write them as we do proper names, noting the corresponding sounds in pictogram language. The *pas* of French negation, for example, will be represented by a footprint (also *pas*).

There are, then, three types of sign in language: the words of the standard vocabulary, proper names, and grammatical words. When we move from the spoken to the written language, we have two possible technical solutions. Either we apply three sets with different graphic signifiers, one for each type of sign, or we use a uniform notation for the sound of all words without regard to the type of sign and without distinguishing which ones stand for concepts, which for individuals, and which for grammatical relations.

This process enables children to understand the principle behind the alphabetical system. But children must be placed in the position of one who has something to communicate in writing in order to truly understand this. They then realize that in order to write 'the fish belonging to Jules', different types of sign are needed for 'Jules', 'fish', and 'the' and 'belonging to'. In other words, to appreciate the constraints of written language one must put oneself in the position of the writer, not that of the reader. Unfortunately, schools put reading before all else. Children in their first year of school are always said to be learning to *read*, not to *write*. It is even more striking that children of 2 are said to be learning to *speak*, not to hear. Written language is received; spoken language is produced.

Of course, reflecting upon the history and function of writing does not replace a syllable exercise or filling a page with the letter a. My point is simply that traditional pedagogy does not seem to give children a grasp of the need for or the advantages of the alphabetical principle.

Pictograms and Syntax

To return to Pierre, my concern was to give him an awareness, if not a clear knowledge, of the special characteristics of the written language. To allow him to appreciate what it is that distinguishes drawing from writing, I asked him, for example, to 'write' a drawing corresponding to 'mouse'. This time he did not produce a pictogram but a drawing of a mouse. When I pointed out to him that his mouse was too detailed, he understood this, tried again, retaining only the mouse's ears and face. He had grasped the principle of *schematic representation*. He had understood that what mattered was to suggest an idea, not to represent an individual by seeking to achieve exact equivalence between the graphic representation and the object.

We enlarged our set of pictograms, building up a collection on sheets of cardboard. In each session we made up statements by placing signs of our choice side by side. He seemed to find the sequences interesting. He was suddenly confronted by the transcription of his own thoughts, but in stabilized form, and this he felt as a liberation from the constraints of attempted verbalization. Gradually he began to see language in a different light. It was clear that until then he had never been able to grasp oral production as something that one could analyse.

I asked him how he might represent a king. He drew a crown. I then suggested that he 'write', using drawings, 'the king is going home'. To the right of the crown he left a space, then placed a pictogram of a door. Lastly, between the crown and the door he placed a blank piece of cardboard and drew an arrow on it.

I pointed out that with the symbols for 'king' and 'door' we could also produce the equivalent of 'the king's house'. To do this we had only to put the drawing of the crown beneath that of the door. At this point his face lit up. Faced with the numerous possible associations between the two drawings (the king of the house, the house of the king, the king in the house…), he came to understand the fundamental role of the *syntax of position* in the construction of a spoken sentence. The spatial arrangement of the written words suddenly justified the word order, both as it concerns the sentence ('Pierre hits Marie' is in no way synonymous with 'Marie hits Pierre') and part of a sentence ('the son of my uncle' is not 'the uncle of my son').

During the same session I felt a need to emphasize the difference between certain items of vocabulary. I drew a fork and pointed out that this drawing could, depending on the context, denote the fork itself as an implement, or the food it enabled one to pick up, or the action of eating, or even a restaurant. Pierre understood then that to express what one wished to transcribe it was necessary to have recourse to additional signs, to non-representative signs, so as to indicate whether the pictogram of the fork meant 'food', 'to eat', or 'restaurant'. In this way he learned to distinguish between nouns, verbs, and complements. In spite of his linguistic difficulties, he had become a grammarian.

Reflection on this subject continued spontaneously and progressed. Pierre noticed that some pictograms were more general in nature than others. An arrow, for example, between a sketch of a child and one of an apple, could mean 'the child takes an apple', 'the child wants an apple', 'the child is throwing the apple away' or 'the child is going towards the apple'. The arrow states the respective roles of the child and the apple, but the nature of the action remains ill defined. This is a sort of phantom pictogram, representing an activity only in the most general way.

Returning to Narrative

The aim of this work was not simply to reflect on the sense of writing. Pierre very soon felt free to use this invented writing system to make new compositions of his own. One day when I was late for one of his sessions and he was rather cross at having to wait, he wrote a statement metaphorically expressing his anger: 'Teddy doesn't like Laurent.' The symbol for teddy bear was followed by a heart crossed out by two large strokes in red. My name was indicated by the letter L. Writing itself had become his. He had spontaneously varied the types of notation: negation, a grammatical tool expressing relation, required a different notation from that of a classic pictogram such as that representing the verb 'to like'. Similarly, my name, being a proper noun, had forced Pierre to write the first letter of a phonetic signifier.

We worked along these lines for a considerable period of time. I would suggest that he construct a sentence, using the pictures we had produced during earlier sessions. When he finished, I would give him an oral translation of whatever I had understood of his statement. If he found my interpretation acceptable, it was my turn to construct a sentence and his to verbalize it.

When writing became a true instrument of exchange, I felt that it was time to tackle the *mechanical* dimension of transcription: the sounds and the division into syllables.

I began by helping Pierre to memorize sequences of words, using writing as a prop. I suggested a game based on a picture book in which each illustration had the corresponding word as its caption. First, Pierre named the objects with the aid of the captions. Then, several pages into the book, I stopped him and suggested that we each draw up a list of all the words we could remember. The words could be written using any kind of symbol, as long as we could both read them. Of course, he began by drawing pictograms. I did not, incidentally, want him to use an alphabetical system: he would have been tempted to transcribe the words he was saying, and would have been unable to, given the way he mispronounced words. Thanks to the use of pictograms, Pierre could memorize a series of syllables, each of which corresponded to a word. But these words were not the words of a sentence. They were already somewhat removed from their context. They were not yet 'pure' series of syllables, but one could make up meaning from them.

As he appeared interested, I decided to work further with sounds. He was the one who offered me the means. From one week to the next he sometimes forgot the meaning of certain pictograms. I therefore suggested to him that he might draw up a list in which he could couple the graphic notation with the alphabetical transcription. A little later he showed me a list of words. The pictograms had disappeared. He had now produced only alphabetical forms. I actively encouraged him to go on keeping lists but was struck by the fact that his lists contained not one grammatical link-word—no articles, prepositions, etc. In order to awaken an interest in words of this kind, I showed him two sentences in which only the preposition was different: 'Jean is coming from the house' and 'Jean is coming to the house'. He understood the difference in meaning, agreed that the preposition was important, but nevertheless declined to include grammatical words in his notebook.

While continuing to stockpile vocabulary, Pierre began writing texts without pictograms. We spent long sessions during which he wrote while I watched in silence. His texts were short and extremely clumsy. The verbs were not conjugated ('He to leave'); the adjectives did not show the gender agreement necessary in French; the nouns bore no indication of the plural.

Since Pierre was fond of music and dancing, during one of these wordless sessions we listened to some Bach. Seeing him with pencil in hand and a sheet of paper in front of him, utterly entranced by the music, I suggested that he write down what he felt. He readily complied, concluding his piece with the appealing phrase 'ça vagabonde' ('nice wandering', based on 'ça va': 'I'm OK'). This was the first time he had described any inner feeling.

A little later Pierre began writing real stories. One day, without warning, while we were still alternating between pictograms and alphabetic writing, I asked him to write a story. I was careful not to stipulate whether it was to be in pictograms or in words. He thought for a moment, then began writing very slowly, using very large letters. When he had finished, I decoded—rather than read in the usual sense of the word—his intended meaning. It was about a boy riding his bicycle in a wood. He was chased by a wolf, fell off his bicycle, and frightened the wolf, who ran away. I said to Pierre that I thought the boy could have scared off the wolf in some other way, without falling off his bicycle. He could have given it a good kick, for example. Pierre smiled.

Slowly his graduation from the spoken to the written word evolved to the point where he was able to develop a story about a dog. This story continued through several episodes, from one session to the next over a period of several months. A transcript of it follows, preserving the spelling of the original. I shall then proceed to analyse certain aspects of it.

Episode I

> Il est une foit
> un cherz a bandon(é)ai/un
> jour un petite garçon le
> trouva/la mene cher lui/
> le dan a mar(ch)gé/il par
> revenu sur le petite garçcon
> plu tard chez lui.

This meant: 'Il était une fois un chien abandonné. Un jour un petit garçon le trouva, l'amena chez lui, lui donna à manger. Il partit, et revint chez le petit garçon plus tard.' (Once there was a stray dog. One day a little boy found it, took it home and fed it. It went away and returned to the little boy's house later.)

This erratic narrative actually observes some of the strictest and most exacting requirements of a literary text. Take, for example, the opening line: 'Il était une fois un chien abandonné.' Pierre announces the general theme of his story. It will deal, he tells us, with what can happen to any abandoned dog. The story proper has not yet begun.

As intended, this theme gives rise to a conflict that will generate the action to follow. A stray dog is a domestic animal, and therefore must belong to somebody. But since this one has been abandoned, nobody knows who its master is. The function of the subsequent narrative is to resolve this predicament.

A second conflict is superimposed upon the first. The real hero is the dog, but it is passive. It is not actively instrumental in the events. The dog is not the one that leaves its master and goes off on its own (unlike Kipling's cat, for example). The dog is the one who is abandoned. In order to manage this situation, Pierre would need the ability to express this contradiction by making the dog the subject of sentences employing the passive voice. But the use of the passive is complicated. Unlike the active voice, the performer of the action is not the subject. To resolve this difficulty, Pierre changes the subject of the second sentence: 'One day a little boy found it.' This time the little boy can be the subject and hero at the same time as being the agent of the action.

With this second sentence we enter the actual time-frame of the narrative. We leave the extra-temporal universe of stray dogs in general to observe a particular situation taking shape, marked by recourse to the adverbial 'one day' and the use of the past historic, among other things.

Yet what follows is somewhat paradoxical as the opening of a narrative. It effectively opens the story at the same time as it closes it: instead of telling of the vicissitudes of the lonely and abandoned dog, Pierre chooses to proceed immediately to its adoption by the little boy. The story could actually end here. When a lost dog finds someone who will take him in, his days as a stray are over. It is usually also the end of the story. Yet this is the point at which Pierre really opens his narrative framework. The chronology is recorded according to the logic of a sequence of actions in the simple past: (le trouva, l'amena chez lui, lui donna à manger . . .).

This leaves the ending: 'It went away and returned to the little boy's house later.' To my mind, this constitutes a conclusion, but this conclusion is complex. On the one hand, it brings a denouement to the events. Thanks to the care lavished upon it by the boy, the stray dog, which up to this point has seemed a passive character in the story, now recovers the ability to act, becoming an individual with the capacity to come and go. But at the same time, the dog's movements back and forth show a degree of instability. It is as if it were hesitating between security with the boy and a hazardous search for its former master. This instability indicates that the resolution proposed in this ending is temporary. It calls for a sequel. Hence the inevitable emergence of conflict, clearly expressed. A dog cannot have two masters. To whom does the dog really belong?

Episode II

> Le mersse le rechèrege le
> son chein/le trouva cherz le
> petite garçon/le mersse le pbad son
> chein/le mersse le dimerci le petite
> garçon/le dans un carbon/le mersse
> il par avec son chein.

This meant: 'Le monsieur recherche son chien, le trouva chez le petit garçon. Le monsieur bat son chien, dit merci le petit garçon, lui donne un cadeau. Le monsieur il part avec son chien.' (The man looks for his dog, and found it with the little boy. The man beats his dog, says thank you little boy, and gives him a present. The man leaves with his dog.)

In the second episode, the dog's first master reappears to reclaim his dog. However, the termination of the connection between the dog and the boy demands a further resolution. First there is the punishment of the dog by its rightful owner (of which we are reminded by the words 'his dog'). Then we hear the words of thanks addressed to the boy. Each of these two actions, moreover, is built according to a fairly rigorous system of balance and contrast. This time the conclusion of the episode is stable. The boy receives compensation for the loss of the dog and the master can leave with a dog that now belongs to him alone.

Episode III

> Le petite garçon le di a
> sa marre peur vaur un bébé
> chein oui car sa peur jouai
> avec ton chein avec la ball
> donné a mancge a ton chein.

This meant: 'Le petit garçon dit à sa mère : "(Est-ce que je peux) avoir un bébé chien?"—"Oui [dit la mère], car tu peux jouer avec ton chien à la balle et donner à manger à ton chien."' (The little boy says to his mother: '[Can I] have a baby dog?'—'Yes [says the mother], you can play ball with your dog and feed it.']

The third episode is indisputably the most confused, both

at the linguistic level and at the level of its overall structure.

The boy's mother intervenes, but she is very different from the earlier protagonists. For one thing, she stands outside the relationship of owner-and-owned with the dog. For another, she is never in direct contact with the dog. The story now takes a new turn; it ceases to be the story of the dog and becomes the story of the little boy. Unhappy at having lost the dog, which had to be returned to its owner, the child tells his mother he would like to have a dog of his own. The story proper is therefore terminated. There are no further events. The text records the words spoken by the little boy.

While the narrative conforms to a very rigorous structure, one cannot help being struck—at least at first—by the faulty syntax. In fact Pierre's grammar observes rules that he applies very strictly, although they are entirely his own.

Since speaking is difficult for him, his syntax is governed by the law of maximum economy. His text contains only what is essential. And what is essential is what modifies the preceding state.

If we accept this simple principle, the structure of each utterance is regular. It applies to the whole text with the exception of the very first statement: 'Once there was a stray dog', and the dialogue between mother and child (where we find different types of statement that stand outside the story proper).

Each of the three episodes comprises a variable number of statements.

The connection between the scenes of an episode is very clear: it is neither the place nor the action that connects the scenes, but rather the hero. Each episode is characterized by the permanent presence of an individual who is Pierre's reference point for the events of each sequence. In this way, even when there is a change of scene within an episode, all the actions described refer to the same agent. There is no need to name the agent before each verb, so, after identifying him at the beginning of an episode, Pierre can use a string of verbs.

This does not, however, mean that Pierre uses no pronouns. All his verbs are preceded by a pronoun, but his use of these is not that of standard French. For Pierre, a pronoun serves to define the verb it precedes. The object pronoun 'le' indicates that the following verb has a complement: 'le trouva'. The pronoun 'il' indicates that the following verb has only a subject: 'il part'. The role of 'le' and 'il' is analogous to that of the articles. In Pierre's thinking, pronouns categorize verbs in the same way as articles categorize nouns.

Thus Pierre's syntactic strategy is very simple. At the beginning of each episode he identifies the agent he is about to speak of (the dog or the little boy). Then in each sequence he relates the actions of this agent, indicating each action by a new verb: 'le trouva', 'l'amena chez lui', 'lui donna à manger'. Each verb is preceded by a pronoun that provides information as to the presence or absence of a complement. If 'le' precedes the verb, it has a complement. If the pronoun preceding the verb is 'il', it has none. The nature of the complement is shown by a noun following the verb.

Everything in the text that is truly part of the narrative follows this pattern, with the exception of one passage only: the point where 'le monsieur' comes to collect his dog from the little boy. Although 'le monsieur' is the subject of the episode, the phrase 'le monsieur' is repeated at the beginning of each statement. The reason is simple. With reference to the couple initially formed by the little boy and the dog, the man represents an external, destabilizing element. 'Le monsieur' is not a natural subject. With each new statement it must be reaffirmed that it is his role to be the agent, although the main character of the piece as a whole is the dog. Pierre's syntax is rigorous and coherent and he owes this in part to his capacity for analysis and ability to reflect upon the function of language.

To this day, it is true, not all of Pierre's problems are resolved. He still has difficulty in expressing himself. But now he can compensate for his difficulties in his exchanges with others. He has just recently embarked on a process of independent self-re-education, and this is helping him to improve his oral production appreciably.

7

What is 'Quality' in Language?

Using specific cases, I have tried to show how speech develops in children who are having difficulty, and how one can sometimes help them learn to express themselves in language of better quality. But what exactly do we mean by 'quality'? It cannot be reduced to an absence of errors, or the range of vocabulary used, or fluent syntax. This is true even if speed in paraphrasing, or the number of meaningful words per sentence indicate a degree of fluency, and all of this is far from unimportant from an academic point of view. Nor can 'quality of language' be restricted to our perspective on the verbal form a person gives to his ideas. Even if a person speaks with the subtlety of a politician or an academic, he may not rise above a very banal level of speech.

I will say, therefore, that good language is first of all a language in which, for all its imperfections, the speaker feels at home. It is true that the more fragmented a language is, the less one feels at home in it. Secondly, good language is language that enables someone else 'to see things'. To paraphrase Arthur Rimbaud's, 'The poet is not one who sees, but one who makes others see,' 'it is not the language of one who sees but a language that enables the other person to see'. Clearly, below a certain level of language development, this is difficult. Moreover, we have heard Pierre, who suffers from a severe disability in his speech, express his feelings while listening to Bach by saying, 'Ça vagabonde.' It is true that the quality of speech is measured by the range of vocabulary and the use of syntax, but this is not enough: speech also entails rhythm and breathing.

Fostering the beginnings of speech means helping it to develop within a system of rules without constraining its poetic dimension. To achieve this it is necessary to be able to listen without understanding everything, or certainly not at first. We need to pay close attention, but without making definite demands, so that gradually the form of speech is adapted to the person it is addressed to, and can develop and diversify. In the end, quality in language matches the definition offered by Leiris, who writes: 'Language: engaging in spirited play'. I remain of the belief that speech is nothing if it fails to invite a listener to join in. To demonstrate this, here are some extracts from a series of exchanges between a well-adjusted 5-year-old girl who speaks well and an adult who is content to listen to the little girl speaking while she draws.

This is a conversation between Rama, who is drawing, and

Mongia, a grown-up friend of the family. The first recording was made at their home in the presence of Rama's younger brother a few days after Christmas 1991. The second and third recordings, of Rama alone, were made on 25 and 29 January 1992. The subjects are both bilingual. They speak Arabic and French, but here use only French.

Rama is aware that she is taking part in something that is beneficial to Mongia, without knowing exactly what the purpose of it all is. She knows that the material collected will be useful for the grown-up 'for her own school', and at once demonstrates eagerness to collaborate, thus making it possible for Mongia to do no more than murmur occasional unobtrusive encourage-ment. I was not present during this series of conversations. Although these were in no sense psychoanalytical sessions, in the adult's calm willingness to listen and in the shared pleasure of this exchange there was something that encouraged the use of language, something similar to those moments which every analyst of children knows from his or her work. At the same time, Rama's gift for fluent development of ideas and her mental health no doubt do more than any therapeutic session to exemplify a mind freely operating between drawing, free association, and narrative, in language of high quality.

Here are some of the key moments.

First Recording: Shortly before Christmas

Rama is seated with a sheet of paper and crayons in front of her. She appears less than sure that she wishes to begin drawing.

RAMA: Snow is white. How do I draw snow?
MONGIA: How do you draw snow?
RAMA: Well, there isn't any white!
MONGIA: That's true, but the paper's white.
RAMA: But if there's white everywhere it isn't snow.
MONGIA: No, it isn't snow.
RAMA: But why is paper always white?

In this first exchange, I am struck by the pointedness of the questions. Rama is asking about the limits of what can be represented in a drawing. Can one depict the whiteness of snow on a white page? How does one depict something that makes no mark? How does one show a void, an absence? To do this, the adult suggests, it is best to leave a blank space. But this is excessively troubling for the child: why should the method proposed contain a display of white, of emptiness? ('Why is paper always white?') The dialogue continues.

RAMA: I'm going to draw Father Christmas.
MONGIA: Good.
RAMA: Father Christmas is red. Where can I find some red?
MONGIA: [*pointing to a red crayon*] There. That one's red.
RAMA: Yep... Father Christmas. Right. He hasn't got any hair, has he?
MONGIA: Hasn't he? What does he have, then?
RAMA: He has a hat because he hasn't got any hair.
MONGIA: Mm... What else has he got?
RAMA: [*commenting one by one on each of the lines as she draws them*] That's his beard. This is the ground, a street... It's very dangerous. Afterwards I'll draw a little girl and then the sun... then some clouds, then the night and the snow. [Pause] Then Father Christmas hides... when he hears a noise. He doesn't hear any noise. He comes down but you can't see him. He's already hiding in the white on the page.

He's going to . . . He's not going to come out again and the little girl will be sad. I'll make her look sad.

To those who might have believed that snow was merely snow this segment of the dialogue brings proof of the opposite: snow is neither a thing nor a shape, but a vanishing place that will eventually swallow up Father Christmas. The narrative, which is remarkable in its structure, provides a kind of dress rehearsal of the theme of disappearance: there is Father Christmas's lack of hair, which, like all absences, is neatly made up for by a hat and a beard. This is followed by a few meteorological attempts to banish the snow, which is symbolic of the void. But Father Christmas nevertheless disappears. Or rather pretends to disappear. He hides, to the great regret of the little girl in the drawing, to whom the artist gives an emotional reaction. It is no longer a straightforward matter of a void and a disappearance, but of a disappearance from the view of an individual, a little girl who is able to express her sadness. Father Christmas does not disappear for nothing: there is somebody there who sees it happen.

Then the drawing settles down, but not for long.

MONGIA: What else would you like to draw?

RAMA: Some flowers. Flowers are yellow, aren't they?

MONGIA: Yes . . .

RAMA: Because I sometimes see yellow flowers. [*Pointing out part of the drawing*] First I go like this. [*Pointing out another part*] This is something. It's a little boat. This is the sea.

MONGIA: Really? Is the sea yellow?

RAMA: No, because I'd like to make it b. . . this colour. Then the flower, which is in the sea. . . Because somebody has thrown it in. A little girl. I'll draw the little girl. You'll see her. Because she has fallen in. She was very pretty. She was poor. Her name was Cinderella.

MONGIA: Oh, I see!

RAMA: There! Her boat has fallen on the water and it's going to break, and we'll see what will happen another day, shall we? Then we'll see.

Here the first session concludes. Disappearance and worry seem to have been finally dispelled. We are left with yellow flowers, stability, and decorative pictures. But again there are signs of a drift into anxiety re-emerging: the flower cannot resist bereavement. It is plucked and flung into the sea. Bereavement also affects the figure of Cinderella, a poor little girl like a poor little flower that is plucked out.

Second Recording: Shortly after Christmas

MONGIA: So what are you going to do?

RAMA: A house...

MONGIA: Mm...

RAMA: Some Christmas things...

MONGIA: Hmm...

RAMA: It's a... It's a ruined house. With no children, no mummies or daddies. Only children.

MONGIA: Mm...

RAMA: And no mummies or daddies, no grannies or anything. The grannies and grandpas are on holiday. A long way away. And the grandpa and granny ... she has come to the big school because she was a baby, she was little and she went to the big school ... She didn't have any friends who were boys. All her friends were girls.

MONGIA: I see.

RAMA: I won't draw the things I said because… because I haven't got much room.

MONGIA: But you have plenty of sheets of paper.

RAMA: All right.

MONGIA: You can do as you like.

RAMA: I can do windows. Can you?

MONGIA: Can I what?

RAMA: Do windows.

MONGIA: Mm…

RAMA: There are some little windows.

MONGIA: Mm…

A strange house this, ruined by all those generations and by people who jostle one another *in absentia*, all those mummies and daddies kept at a distance from a place inhabited by a spontaneous generation of children without begetters. And what power of negation, which enables Rama to make an assertion at the same time as its opposite! Let us continue.

RAMA: This is a star because… because it's Christmas.

MONGIA: Good. And what's that?

RAMA: A girl who's 3, 6 today. Her birthday isn't today. When she's 5½ that's her birthday.

MONGIA: Mm… I see.

RAMA: Her hair's like that because it's been cut.

MONGIA: Mm…

RAMA: This is a girl like you. How old are you?

MONGIA: I'm 6.

RAMA: She's 6 too.

MONGIA: So we're the same age.

RAMA: So am I. After I've been 5½ I'll be 6 and when I'm 6 it'll be my birthday.

MONGIA: Mm…

RAMA: Isn't it true? Because Mummy told me… She has a nice dress… When it's my birthday how old will you be?

MONGIA: You'll be 6.

RAMA: Yes, but when it's my birthday how old will you be?

MONGIA: On your birthday I'll be as old as I am [*laughs*].

RAMA: Why?

MONGIA: Why? Because we weren't born on the same day. All right, now will you tell me what this is?

RAMA: But I've already told you. It's a house and a star and a girl.

MONGIA: Mm…

RAMA: What are your children's names when you take them out of your tummy? What'll they be called? Choose some names!

MONGIA: Oh, I don't know.

RAMA: Choose the names of your children, that you'll take out of your tummy! Choose their names!

MONGIA: I don't know. I… I… I'll think about it.

RAMA: All right. I'll tell you something: you'll call your children the same as us: the boy will be Somer and the girl Rama.

MONGIA: All right…

RAMA: All right?

MONGIA: All right.

In the previous scene, where the children were conceived spontaneously, as here with the birthday, the question of birth and babies reappears. But the anguish, no doubt all too keenly felt, brings on a shift in levels: the narrative mode is abandoned. The little girl breaks off her story and speaks directly to the adult, asking, 'When it's my birthday how old will you be?' This question marks a temporary lapse by Rama into prelogical thought. The memory of birth—every child's first experience of separation—creates in Rama an anxiety that she resolves by linking her own birthday to that of the grown-up, in order to try to counter the separation experienced at birth, when her body was detached from that of her mother. Seeing how astonished the adult is, Rama modifies her story and suggests that Mongia should have two imaginary children, one of whom, a girl, will also be called Rama. This is a return to the narrative mode, but it is a narrative in which resemblances to living persons are far from coincidental!

RAMA: Because there's no Rama; there's two mummies with two mummies' names, but not the same.

MONGIA: And what's that girl's óname?

RAMA: Cinderella.

MONGIA: Cinderella. And what has happened to her?

RAMA: But not like the other Cinderella. She's 6 and it's hard to . . .

MONGIA: Do you know her story?

RAMA: Nope. She's telling a story to her house.

MONGIA: And what sort of story is she telling?

RAMA: It's her mummy . . . because it's a little house . . . She's talking to it.

MONGIA: What is she saying?

RAMA: She's telling a story.

MONGIA: And what is the story she's telling?

RAMA: It's the story of Snow White.

MONGIA: And do you know that story? I don't.

RAMA: Oh yes, I know it but I can't remember it.

MONGIA: What about the story of Cinderella?

RAMA: Yes. I don't remember it either.

MONGIA: What is this girl saying to her mummy?

RAMA: She's saying, 'Mummy for my birthday you could buy me some nice earrings and a nice shiny dress,' and she goes to buy a magic wand and then, after that, she makes her a very pretty dress, and then it was this one, the nice dress.

MONGIA: Mm...

RAMA: And her daddy's gone on holiday.

MONGIA: Mm...

RAMA: Not on holiday now, but he was on holiday before. Now he's not on holiday any more.

MONGIA: He's back?

RAMA: Yes.

MONGIA: Mm...

RAMA: He was working.

MONGIA: Working on holiday?

RAMA: Yes. That's his daughter there.

MONGIA: Ah! So it's her sister?

RAMA: Yes, her little sister. Two little sisters. They're pretty. They're sisters, not ... They're not mummies.

MONGIA: I see. They're sisters.

RAMA: They're little sisters.

If there are two Ramas, the one telling the story and the one invented in the story, why shouldn't there be two mummies? And furthermore, why not invert the movement from reality to fiction by making one of the two mummies able to have a daughter who has the name of a well-known fairy-tale? This is a two-way exchange between reality and fiction, deploying mirrors and parallels that offer a fictitious resolution of the painful problem of separation. If (separated) people were as like as two peas, why should we not imagine that there is no longer any difference, any distinction, any separation? That children should no longer have to suffer from the absence of their mothers because they would be exact replicas of them? But separation does exist. Mothers exist. And Rama cannot simply confine herself to clones.

Now Rama is drawing a crown.

RAMA: This is the mummy's crown. The mummy is also called 'princess'. She isn't sad but she does it on purpose, you know... She doesn't do it on purpose because sometimes she cries, she's not crying here, she's laughing, but... because she's hurt herself... She's hurt herself because...she's had a bump, she fell and bumped her knee and it bled, the poor mummy... She's laughing, do you see? She's not crying because she didn't hurt herself. Her daughter doesn't know what her mummy was doing.

Here Rama's language falters, affected by some emotion whose cause cannot be clearly discerned. It is possible that Rama is in the process of telling us, in connection with her drawing, about a traumatic event from her life (the blood, the mother falling down). Mongia, the grown-up, must be made a witness to the event in order for the sense of tragedy to abate. At first any suggestion of pain is instantly rejected (laughing/crying, deliberately/accidentally), giving a chaotic sequence. Later, as the story takes shape, we see an orderly juxtaposition of opposites. This structure is not a consequence of the fear experienced by Rama, the narrator. Rather it is the effect of deliberate hesitation built into the thought patterns of the protagonist. Then the theme of white recurs.

RAMA: What colour do you want? It's your turn to choose a colour now.
MONGIA: No, it's your turn.
RAMA: What's that? I'm not quite sure...
MONGIA: That's white.
RAMA: Perhaps it'll do. We'll see. No, I don't like white. Put the ones that don't work here. I'll put the white one here with the others. It works. I'll change it. This is grass, and a sheet of paper. That's the sheet of paper, right, or else it's the drawing on the paper.

MONGIA: Mm. What are all the other things?

RAMA: A sun. I'll do it, I can do it. Sometimes the sun hurts your eyes. No, it doesn't hurt your eyes, but even so the sun says something like… Afterwards it's the sun on the sheet of paper. I've finished.

Immediately after the mother has had her fall, Rama returns to the theme of white and disappearance. This constructs a retrospective echo of the initial theme evoked in the first dialogue. At the beginning of this dialogue, we can see how her problem with white anticipates the question of the mother's fall. However, after the white comes the sun.

RAMA: Oh yes, there's this big house in the sea. It's drawn with big lines. It's not big, but still it's like this. It's my friend Sabine's house. It's my friend Bénédicte's house. My friend Laure, you know, didn't go skating because she cut herself. She was bleeding so she got some sweets. She doesn't want give any of them to anyone because she cut herself. My teacher said, 'Don't give anybody any.' I've got some sweets. I can… I want to take one because I can't read them.

No doubt it is a powerfully felt sadness that leads Rama to insert real names into scenes which are otherwise imagined. She introduces a memory from her real life, a memory that she recounts as a story, to ward off the fiction that preceded it, too pregnant with psychological truth. The story is no doubt more real, but less true.

These, then, are the thoughts I might have had if I had been in Mongia's place and if Rama and I had been engaged in a task based on language. The poetry of this child's text, the sharp clarity of the twists and turns in her narrative seem to me to provide a particularly apposite illustration of language of high quality. All we have to do is listen.

Conclusion

This book owes its origins to a fact which has been established and reiterated many times, but which is nevertheless strange and to which I wished to bring my own experience: there are children who reach the age of 4 or 5, sometimes even 6 or 7, without speaking, and who take off spectacularly within one year simply by meeting an adult for half an hour two or three times a week. This is a fact that requires an explanation. The study of each case history allows us to make progress in addressing the questions that exercise linguists, neurologists, and psychoanalysts alike.

Which processes will work, and with which children? Even if some children who did not speak suddenly begin talking, this is no reason for great rejoicing. For one thing, not all children begin to speak. Some autistic children, for example, never speak. Moreover, among those who do, some will continue to have very serious difficulties in expressing themselves. Last and most important, speech is not an end in itself. Speech is a necessary condition but not a sufficient condition of psychological health, and to me, as an analyst, it is psychological health that matters.

Is it possible to identify, with the benefit of hindsight, what it was that made a form of treatment beneficial?

I will restrict myself to a few common-sense observations. First, the younger a child is the greater the chances of successful treatment. This is self-evident. But when should one begin? Before the age of 2 there is no reason for anxiety if a child does not speak, as long as it babbles and gets on well with other people. After the age of 3 it is often advisable to take action, and the sooner one begins, the better.

Age apart, the other factors that make for successful treatment are linked with what is usually termed the responsiveness of the child. When something—however fleeting, rudimentary, or abstract—becomes established in the sessions with the specialist, possibilities are opened; for example, when children begin to show signs of reacting to something the specialist says or does in response to one of their own endeavours. This implies that the main blockage to language development lies much closer to *the wish to build contacts with others* than to real difficulties of expression.

In order to proceed beyond these few common-sense observations, one must indulge in generalizations. I myself have always tried to emphasize the difference between one form of treatment and another, for even if certain characteristic difficulties recur and coincide, and if, with time, certain identifiable types of child emerge, it is very important to see what constitutes the particular character of each case, of each individual.

The question then arises of knowing what will work in the treatment of a particular child. I would not wish to prescribe—nor could I prescribe—some cut-and-dried recipe, the use of a single method which might be supplemented by some wiring diagrams of the cerebral circuits. I do not believe in panaceas. Nor do I believe in miracles. This kind of treatment of children requires no special gift or mystical tendency. It entails a certain attitude, a way of being—a certain professional posture which one might, following Descartes, call 'provisional'—which prevents one from being locked into a system. Even if certain principles exist, we should not be content to simply follow them without any creative improvisation.

In fact, while all kinds of difficulties are encountered in work of this nature, in my view the greatest is the need to be constantly inventive. What works with one child will not necessarily work with another, even if the two seem to present comparable problems. Conversely, if something succeeds with the first and one wishes to draw on it for the second, this is certainly not a consequence of pure chance or sheer laziness. The difficulty lies in extracting the principle that was successfully applied in the first case, while shedding the particular features that applied in that case alone. To do this one must constantly analyse the child's responses to suggestions. It is necessary to understand why the child responds to certain things and not to others.

I believe that this is a requirement that lies at the heart of all therapeutic work. We find it in both psychotherapy and speech therapy.

But there is one difficulty of a more specific nature associated with my own style of practice. If two facts, two events occur one after the other during a single session, how should they be interpreted? When should we explain things in terms of cognition, wording, or psychic processes? Of course, this question does not arise *during* the session, as I am then obliged to rely on intuition; but the problem surfaces later, when I reflect on what took place in the session with the child. And the answer is not easily found. In general, once the session has developed a certain continuity, when it no longer consists of disconnected points (playing with play-dough, then doing some drawing, then looking at a book, then looking out into the street), as soon as we can find some meaning in the variations of activities and within the episodes making up these variations, it seems to me that the psychoanalytical method is the most creative approach to spontaneous play and possible interpretation of that play.

One final question arises: the termination of treatment. Should treatment end when we feel we have provided the child with access to language? Here too it is difficult to give a cut-and-dried answer. But in most cases the answer is no. If neurological or cognitive problems are not solely responsible for the inability to speak, the development of speech will no doubt stabilize certain psychological functions, while serving to bring out conflicts that previously the child could not really imagine. It therefore seems necessary to help the child face—and to some extent struc-ture—these conflicts before leaving them to their own devices.

Once we admit that language is part of the symbolic functioning of human beings, all speech therapy can be seen to be in part psychotherapy. And the question of the termination of treatment is then posed in terms analogous to those of child psychiatry. The treatment of a child who does not speak does not end on the day that the child begins to speak, but when the child can say what it wishes to say, the day when it learns to 'lie truthfully', like the rest of us.

Some Ideas from the Back of my Mind

While working with a child, I have a number of ideas at the back of my mind concerning language, its effects on thought and the way in which it connects with other human faculties. Having considered a variety of particular situations and the way that I experienced them, I would like to turn my attention to some of these ideas.

Language is situated at the nexus of three orders of data. These are: the perception of the outside world and the way this is processed by the brain (the cognitive pole); the transformation of thoughts into words (the mechanics of speech, the aphasic pole); and the expression of wishes with regard to others (the symbolic pole). Each of these registers places its stamp on language. We see this in the regular patterns that recur from one language to another, as well as in the historical evolution of each language. We have been able to see, in the cases of Fabien, Rachid, Kim, and the others, the extent to which access to language depends on each of these registers.

The Cognitive Field: Perception and Interaction

Clearly the way humans apprehend the world about them, the way they picture it to themselves, organize it, and adapt to it, influences various aspects of their language. Side by side with the automatic systems that control our relations with our natural environment, there are others, just as fundamental, that regulate our relations with other people, and these have an equally important influence on language.

Recent studies of perception allow us to define some general principles. First, with senses such as sight and hearing, the same methods are not deployed to perceive all objects; different strategies are used, which vary according to the object to be perceived. The brain does not approach the recognition of faces and that of knives and forks in the same way. There are those who are unable to recognize familiar faces, although they can unfailingly distinguish a knife from a fork.

However, all strategies follow the same general principles. First, a sense such as sight or hearing does not produce a copy of the outside world. On the contrary, the basic outline of an object is first determined, then those elements that stand out from it. As when putting together an identikit picture, after establishing the general outline of the face we focus on certain salient details (eyes, mouth, nose, ears). Then, for each of these features, we have the choice of various profiles stored in the memory: rounded or pointed ears, a straight nose or a hooked one.

The way we perceive and deal with the world has undeniable effects upon the structure of language. Take the use of the singular and the plural, for example. The fact that we naturally say 'some tables' but less naturally 'some waters' bears some relation to the way we deal with reality. When we handle a table we know where it begins and ends. With water this is far from the case.

In the same way, to describe a picture, the reference point of the statement is partially based on the reference point that the eye selects. The eye begins with the stable components, then fixes the others. If there is a ball under a bed, we notice the bed first. It serves as a frame by which we locate the ball. In the corresponding statement we would say 'the ball is under the bed', rather than 'the bed is above the ball'. The bed, being more stable than the ball, provides a visual point of reference that is retained in language.

However, the dependence of language on perception is not total. Let us look again at the plural. It is true that we do not naturally say 'some waters', but it can be said in certain contexts, just as we can talk about 'some wines' if we wish to differentiate their quality and their origin. Linguistic categories are not watertight. Without denying the influence of the cognitive, we cannot claim that it is all-important in language. There is no linear causal relationship between cognition and grammatical categories.

The Effects of Cognitive Difficulties

There are cases in which the effect of perception is incontestable in language. The ability to call up a mental image, to transform it, to find our bearings in a place that we know, to know what to expect, to reconstruct a continuous film from still pictures, is a cognitive function whose importance may sometimes be assessed by its absence.

Once in a session with an educated young man of about 20, whom I was treating for some ill-defined cognitive difficulties, we were working with a guessing game. To the question, 'What is a weathercock?' the young man confessed ignorance. Yet he knew the figurative meaning of this word, as he was able to say that it meant 'somebody who is changeable'. Paradoxically, however, the primary meaning eluded him. Conjecturing that the problem arose from a difficulty in identifying the place where one might find a weathercock, I asked if it would be found indoors or outside. 'Outside,' he said, without hesitation. I tried to contextualize further by asking, 'High up or low down?' 'High up,' he said.

Then he added spontaneously, 'Isn't it a cockerel... up there? Yes, that's it! The fog has cleared. I can see the cockerel on a church roof.'

This young man had difficulty in finding his bearings amidst a myriad of mental images, and this had a direct effect on his ability to access the meaning of words that he knew.

The ability to construct what one might call an evolving mental representation on a fixed base is also a cognitive prerequisite for understanding certain forms of language, such as that used in comic strips. This same young man and I were once reading *Tintin in America*. In a sequence of three pictures, Tintin was shown buying a cowboy suit. We first saw him looking in a shop window, then he was inside the shop, in front of a mirror, trying on a suit. The bubble read, 'This one will do very nicely.' In the third picture, Tintin was leaving the shop with a package under his arm. Although he had read and grasped the meaning of the words and all the pictures, the young man could not understand that the hero had bought some new clothes. He was not making the connection between one picture (Tintin in the tailor's shop) and the one before (Tintin outside the shop) recognizing that these converged in one 'idea' (Tintin buying some new clothes). Each picture remained self-contained and he was unable to construct the mental representations that would have enabled him to establish a link between the drawings. Here some mild cognitive difficulties had an effect on a particular kind of written communication.

Cognitive Prerequisites in Relationships

The cognitive register is not only applied in the way humans relate to the world. It also comes into play in the relations human beings construct among themselves.

To communicate with others it is necessary to produce and understand signs relayed by facial expressions. Emotions expressed, and the direction of one's look, indicate the object of interest.

The ability to read the facial expressions of another person means that one recognizes that person as a thinking individual. It also provides information concerning the emotional value of what that person has to communicate. At the same time, the direction of that person's gaze enables us to understand what is to be the subject of the exchange, and to find some common ground. Similarly, the gesture of pointing requires the ability to direct one's eyes and one's finger. But above all, pointing means indicating something to somebody in order to convey an idea that is associated with that thing. Extending a finger towards a pencil is not simply to point it out. It may mean, 'That pencil reminds me of the drawing I did the other day while you were watching.' Like directing one's gaze, or laughing, pointing is a cognitive faculty that can quickly acquire a symbolic function. This happens as soon as the subject comes to interpret the signs seen in their conversation partner as a measure of intentions that are analogous to their own. It sometimes happens that this natural cognitive aptitude is lost and it is necessary to relearn not so much the gesture as the fact that it has meaning for others.

Verbalization: The Passage from Ideas to Words

By 'verbalization' I mean the mechanism that enables us to move from words to ideas and from ideas to words, and allows us to indicate through discontinuous elements a form of thought, representation, or emotion that is itself continuous. In short, a mechanism that produces sounds in sequence. Moreover it is possible to see in it an essential feature of human communication. 'The need for an orderly arrangement of sounds,' wrote Jacob Grimm in *On the Origin of Language*, 'compels us to divide them and connect them.' Here lies a defining characteristic of human language: it is articulated. Grimm links this intuition with the qualifier merops, as applied to humans by Homer: 'Oi meropes, meropes anthropoi oi brotoi' (a human being is one who can divide and articulate the sounds that come out of his mouth). What defines human language it not simply its symbolic function, but also the division and articulation of the signifier. I will now focus on this latter aspect, which includes the representation of continuous thoughts by discontinuous signifiers, the process of encoding thoughts into speech chains and the decoding of speech chains into thoughts.

The Two Circuits and Two Types of Energy

Since the days of Jackson and Freud we have become accustomed to a schematic representation of the functioning of language by a dual opposition. First, one of circuits. A series of words may follow either an 'automatic' or a 'voluntary' circuit. Swearwords belong on the automatic side, the formulation of ideas on the voluntary side. Second, there is the circuit of energies, in which the opposition is between the emotional and the motor functions. The speech apparatus may be activated either by an emotion or an action.

Automatic speech corresponds to a kind of reflex that operates when prompted by emotion or to accompany a ritual action. It requires a particularly high level of energy and produces only a limited number of set expressions, such as swearwords or polite phrases. It does not involve true representation. No doubt it is this circuit that enabled Kim, who had severe aphasia, to exclaim 'What-non-sense!' in a clear and finely modulated voice whenever I did something she judged inappropriate. The force of her displeasure facilitated its phonetic and melodic expression and prompted an automatic verbalization. Her words were a direct reaction to a situation, not the expression of a thought. At most they lent a verbal contour to a sensation.

Another instance of automatic verbalization, this time in the register of motor function, may be seen at the moment when Kim, prompted by a handshake and the opening of the office door, had no difficulty in saying to me, 'Till next time.' Although this was a moment of some emotion, which must have exerted considerable influence, the articulation of these words was certainly stimulated above all by a ritual motor function (our handshake and the opening of the door). It is actions that activate language. Although the utterance was more than a simple motion of the speech organs, its meaning was not yet fully formed. It would become more so when I could bring her to imagine our next session. The words would therefore take on new meaning retrospectively. The vague sense of separation would become connected to real representations.

Voluntary speech is different. It converts a representation into words. The energy that must be mobilized derives from what is suggested by the representation. Thus children who are thinking of their teddy bear, for example, will reflect in their pronunciation of the word the emotional pleasure associated with this toy. They will be happy to say the word in order to extract from the phonetic action a pleasure comparable to that which they would derive from the teddy itself. The pleasure linked with the representation supplies the energy required to pronounce the word.

In the sphere of motor function, voluntary speech is based on an action that is associated with the referent (the object referred to) to assist verbalization. The more the referent can be manipulated, the easier it is to remember its name. We can see this in patients affected by the inability to recall a word. When asked to put names to objects shown to them in pictures, these patients have less difficulty in producing the name of a hammer or a fork than in the case of objects no less concrete but not associated with any action: a tree, a cloud, or the sun. We may note in passing that certain abstract objects may be manipulated indirectly: geometric figures such as circles, squares, and triangles are abstractions, but their shape is the product of specific movements; this means that it is easier for some patients to find the word 'square' than the word 'tree'.

The Organization of the Lexicon in the Mind

The formulation of a thought depends, of course, on the store of vocabulary in the mind, that is, on what constitutes the mental lexicon. Today it is thought that this vocabulary evolves during the course of development. To start with, when a child says a word that stands for a whole sentence, this may be seen in one of two ways. Either the child replicates the general melody of the statement and the pronunciation of the syllables remains approximate; the child has retained the tune but not the words; or the child focuses on the principal consonant of the keyword and does its best to replicate it. This opposition confirms the hypothesis of the two forms of energy required for speech: children who remember the melody use only a memory linked with a sensation, an emotion; those children who focus on the dominant consonant favour the phonetic gesture and the motor function. Then, of course, each child develops the two modes.

For a long period, the vocabulary is built solely on meaning. The signifiers that correspond to a given sphere of activity evoke others and form networks: 'shovel' suggests 'rake', 'castle' suggests 'sand', etc. Words that produce similar impressions also become associated with one another: 'honey' suggests 'sun', 'warmth', 'softness', etc. But when the number of words reaches about fifty, things change. We can see this if we observe the faults in pronunciation of a child who has no linguistic difficulty. In a vocabulary of under fifty words, faults are fairly rare. The child is content to reduce words that are too long to their first or last syllable. With a number in excess of fifty, the number of syllables is respected, but systematic simplification appears: lapin (rabbit), until now pronounced 'pin', is suddenly pronounced 'papin'.

The nature of these distortions is so systematic that computer simulations have been built on them. It appears that, beyond a certain threshold, the memory becomes saturated and a reorganization of the system becomes necessary. The reorganization is simple. The basis is no longer the storage en bloc of signifiers, but rather the construction in each case of a hierarchy of increasingly specific information: the number of syllables, the dominant consonant (the one that shapes the framework, the root), and lastly the other syllables. Each time speakers wish to use a word, they begin by reprocessing it, reconstructing it on the basis of this series of data. Incidentally, this is the sequence we follow when recovering a word that we have on the tip of our tongue: we first recall the number of syllables, then a salient consonant, and the word is suddenly resurrected. This also explains why a child will start saying 'babbit' (for rabbit) at the point where the vocabulary is being reorganized. The need to form a hierarchy of information about the signifier suddenly requires us to work harder if we are to pronounce it correctly. Initially, the first level of the hierarchy is respected—the number of syllables, then the second—the value of the salient consonant. But the information stored at the last level, about the other syllables, is disregarded.

The new arrangement has the advantage of permitting much faster access to vocabulary, owing to a classification of words within each 'zone of meaning', according to the number of syllables and salient consonants. But the disadvantage is that a further stage is required before the rediscovered word can be pronounced, since the search for the word no longer leads to a signifier ready for use, but rather to a collection of data out of which the signifier must be reassembled before we open our mouths. This is the point at which children make mistakes.

But the most serious failure occurs when the reorganization of the mental vocabulary at fifty words does not take place. The child then possesses only the classification provided by meaning. The search for a word becomes extremely complicated, and in order to simplify it, the child's range of lexical networks is restricted. One dominant word is used in all circumstances. Thus, during one session, a little girl looked into the box of toys and said clearly 'Kleenex!', although the box contained no paper hankies. I pointed this out to her but she insisted. I was puzzled by this, and said to her, 'Take the Kleenex out, then.' She immediately pulled out a toy chamber pot. A moment later she took a giraffe and sat it on the pot. I realized then that 'Kleenex' actually meant the pot as well as any other item from the series 'poo, pot, paper', as long as it belonged in the sphere of personal hygiene. The Kleenex, the pot, the moment of defecation, and the matter of potty-training were all connected by the girl's use of the word 'Kleenex'. In fact, she was not using the wrong word. But she had only the one word to designate a whole range of objects and ideas. Furthermore, when she used the word 'Kleenex' to denote the pot, she had no sense of this as a mistake.

The Influence of the Cognitive on the Mechanics of Speech

As we have seen in the case of this little girl, when the mechanics of speech fail to structure the vocabulary, the cognitive sphere reclaims control. This applies equally in patients suffering from aphasia. During a course of treatment, a man who was asked what a razor was used for replied, 'A razor is a rake, for scraping.' The form of the signifier 'ras + oir' did not lead him towards the root that is common to this and related words. In formulating his reply, he made no reference to the verb raser (to shave) or the noun rasage (shaving). Nor did he resort to the realistic scene of shaving in the morning in front of the bathroom mirror. To him, the word first suggested a sensation comparable to that of scratching (griffer) or scraping (gratter). This is the impression that determined his description of the function of the implement. It is a physical sensation linked to both an action and a complex bodily experience: the clenched hand, the scratching and smarting of the razor, the similarity in form between a safety razor and a rake, the motion to and fro over the skin like that of a rake smoothing gravel. Through these lexical excursions, this man provides us with the connotative associations that words can suggest when removed from any context. In all this primitive diversity, the cognitive sphere, and sometimes the poetic sphere, have a part to play.

The Symbolic Pole: Why Speak at All?

Given the ease with which a little baby succeeds in getting what it wants without saying a word, one may wonder why one day we should feel a need to speak. What is the use of it?

To this question, there are two current answers, neither of which I find satisfactory. The first says that we speak to get what we want; the other, that we speak to construct some sort of picture, a phonetic copy of reality. The first response is unsatisfactory because it serves better as a definition of exclamations and facial expressions than of speech. Monkeys can also get what they want. The second is equally unsatisfactory because we usually address somebody who can see what we see, and I have never understood why we should use words to imitate a reality that our conversation partner may observe directly. The idea of language as an expression of needs is as difficult to justify as that which sees it as an exact copy of reality.

In one sense, it is clear that speech is only necessary when one must indicate to another person something that is not apparent to that person. But without a context, indicating something that someone else cannot see is an impossible task: there is no limit to the number of topics, and one can never be sure of making oneself fully understood. How is one to turn the mind of one's interlocutor in the desired direction? How is one to find a reference point that is sufficiently stable and firmly shared? The answer is simple: the basis of the exchange must be the situation in which the discourse takes place. In order to say things that cannot be seen, if we wish to be understood, we must find a basis in things that can be seen. The function of language is to express the invisible by starting from what is visible to all parties. It is not based on constructing copies of what is visible. Nor is it completely detached from the visible.

Anticipation and Retrospection

It remains to define this invisible thing that language makes manifest and that it connects with the visible. Briefly stated, we can say that it is thoughts that give meaning to reality.

We are often surprised, plunged into a state of stupefaction, or so stunned by reality that we are left speechless, unable to understand or even express what we feel. Like Roquentin in the famous scene in the park in *La Nausée*, when his thought processes break down as he looks at the tree and its root, for want of words to express them, we confront a silent new world. Only a return to the use of language enables us to emerge from our stupor. By speaking again, we can focus and classify a reality that ceases to be an amorphous mass, and we can structure a representation that allows us to give meaning to what we see.

I have mentioned Roquentin, but I could just as well have taken the little bear from *Goldilocks and the Three Bears*. In that story, Baby Bear, on returning from his walk, finds his bowl empty on the table. At first he is dumbfounded. To him, the empty bowl is an object that cannot be explained, a piece of scrap metal. Then he recovers his

wits and exclaims, 'Who's been eating my porridge?' The verbalization
of his surprise at once builds a scenario that gives meaning to what
he sees, even if this meaning is a source of deep displeasure to the
hungry young bear. To a baby bear, an empty bowl constitutes a
reality bereft of meaning. The only coherent reality would be a bowl
full of steaming porridge. To give back meaning to reality he must
reinvent the story that will allow him to re-establish the connection
between a full bowl and an empty one, that is, to invent the story
of the empty bowl. In other words, he can only escape from the
absurd by describing the reality and giving it meaning. This meaning,
moreover, is not an objective property. In itself, an empty bowl is not
more empty of soup than it is of cocoa or anything else. It is simply
empty. Also, in order to say that a bowl is empty, one must expect to
find it full. We do not say that a bowl stored in a cupboard is empty.
It is simply a bowl. Thus, to describe a bowl as empty of porridge is
to invest it with meaning, but with meaning in the eyes of a particular
individual—in this case, in the eyes of Baby Bear, who structures the
disparity between what he sees (the empty bowl) and what he wants
(a bowl of porridge).

In addition to this function of retrospective categorization, speech
also enables us to express our desires. But we should be careful not to
allow this definition to present language as a kind of cry of discomfort.
Indeed, a cry manifests displeasure or an appeal for help, a request.
Speech may be all of these. But it is more. Above all it permits the
speaker to clarify for him or herself what he or she lacks, and to
picture it to himself. If, faced with his empty bowl, Baby Bear were to
exclaim, 'I want some more porridge!', he would certainly be voicing a
request. But above and beyond this, while speaking, he would realize
that he wanted something and that here was a wish that should not
(yet) be taken for reality.

Whether it expresses retrospective categorization or anticipation,
language imposes its coherence upon reality without mistranslating

whatever causes disappointment to the subject. It makes tensions
bearable, but does not cancel them. That is where its symbolic effect
lies.

Some Last Questions

The linguist Manfred Bierwisch was in the habit of saying that any
slip of the tongue presupposed at once a failure in the mechanism
that manages the processing of thoughts into words and an adoption
of the malfunction as part of the conflicts of the mind. Each of
the two dimensions has been absorbed and taken for granted, the
one in psycholinguistics, the other in psychoanalysis. What is less
commonplace is an insistence on the link between them. In all thought
expressed by language, there are several orders of phenomena that are
radically different from one another yet connected. There is that which
is related to symbolization (the way we may process our thoughts, the
connection between what we want and what we see, the relation we
establish between our own thoughts and those of others), and there
is that which refers to the way the brain constructs or interprets a
series of sounds. I do not for a moment suggest that psychoanalysts
are interested solely in the symbolizing function of language and that
linguists deal only with the mechanical aspect. I do not believe that
this is the case. Linguists and psychoanalysts alike are interested in
the processes and the symbolic operations of which language is the
manifestation. Symbolization, that which bears on the representation
of absence, on metaphor, is as much the concern of the linguist as
of the psychoanalyst, although, of course, their approaches remain
different.

I also believe that both are equally convinced of the need to attend
to the mechanics of speech, for what is the effect on thought of a
malfunctioning speech apparatus? Children whose imaginations tend

to brim over, for example, who have swirling fantasies or thoughts a little too unstable and volatile, would no doubt be soothed and focused if their speech apparatus were more resistant, firmer, and if it enabled them to produce better-structured language. Frequently, moreover, the same children have difficulty finding certain words for objects, and so replace them with 'thingummy', and we can see them stumbling over words that are somewhat too long or too difficult. Would not a stronger linguistic apparatus provide a barrier for them against the ceaseless onrush of their thoughts? If they were better armed as a *merops*, would they not be better able to shape their expression into a more connected narrative in which repression, for example, might be better equipped to play its part, and integrative development could proceed more easily?

In extreme cases, when the speech apparatus has never functioned well, the question of consequences for the symbolizing function is squarely posed. What can become of the symbolizing capacity (I deliberately say 'symbolizing' rather than 'fantasizing'; I mean the capacity to metaphorize, to represent absence) in a 6-year-old whose speech consists of juxtaposed keywords and can only say 'cow, dead' instead of 'the cow has died'? And conversely, what are the repercussions of this juxtaposition of words upon the individual who is symbolizing? In the worst case, do not children who speak in keywords become used to employing language in a way that prevents them from taking the time to think? When we have difficulty in finding the words we need and putting them together, are we not necessarily reduced to a form of violence, or, on the contrary, a form of withdrawal into oneself, or condemned to repetitive actions? Whatever the case, these are questions that clinical practice demands that we ask.

Bibliography

Titles are arranged by field. Only essential works and collections are listed, but some particularly innovative articles have been included.

LANGUAGE ACQUISITION

BLOOM, L. *One Word at a Time: The Use of Single Word Utterances Before Syntax* (New York: Mouton, Hawthorne, 1983).

—— (ed.), *Readings in Language Development* (New York: Wiley, 1978).

BOUTON, L., *Le Développement du langage: Aspects normaux et pathologiques* (Paris: Presses de l'UNESCO, Masson, 1980).

BRONCKART, J. P., MALRIEU, P., SIGUAN-SOLER, M., SINCLAIR DE ZWART, H., SLAMA-CAZACU, T., and TABOURET-KELLER, A., *La Genèse de la parole* (Paris: Presses universitaires de France, 1977).

BROWN R., *A First Language, The Early Stages* (Cambridge, Mass.: Harvard University Press, 1973).

BRUNER, J. S., 'From Communication to Language: A Psychological Perspective', *Cognition*, 3 (1970), 255–87.

FRANÇOIS, F., 'Eléments de linguistique appliqués à l'étude du langage de l'enfant', *Cahiers Baillère*, Orthophonie, 6 (Paris, 1978).

MENUYK, P., *The Acquisition and Development of Language* (Englewood Cliffs, NJ: Prentice Hall, 1971).

Moscato, M., and Piéraut-Le Bonniec, G. (eds.), *Le Langage: Construction et actualisation*, Publications de l'Université de Rouen, 98 (1989), 19–38.

EARLY COGNITION AND SKILL DEVELOPMENT, NEUROPSYCHOLOGY

'Le Cerveau et l'Intelligence', *Science et Vie*, suppl. ser. 177 (1991).

'Emergence du cognitif', *Le Débat*, special edn. (Paris: Gallimard, 1989).

Fodor, J., *The Modularity of Mind* (Cambridge, Mass.: MIT Press, 1983).

Frith,U., *Autism: Explaining the Enigma* (Oxford: Blackwell, 1989).

Gibello, G., 'Dysharmonies cognitives. Dyspraxies, dysgnosies, dyschronies: des anomalies de l'intelligence qui permettent de lutter contre l'angoisse dépressive', *Revue de Neuropsychiatrie Infantile*, 9 (1976), 439–52.

Huber, G., 'Intentionnalité et scénario dans les sciences cognitives et la psychanalyse', *Penser-Apprendre. La Cognition chez l'enfant. Les Troubles de l'apprentissage. La Prise en charge*, Les Colloques de Bobigny (Paris: Eshel, 1988), 130–5.

Luriia, A. R., *Higher Cortical Functions in Man*, trans. from the Russian by B. Haigh, (London: Tavistock, 1966).

Mehler, J., and Duroux, E., *Naître humain* (Paris: Odile Jacob, 1995).

Ninio, J., *L'Empreinte des sens* (Paris: Odile Jacob, 1989).

Pinol-Douriez, M., 'Fantasy Interactions or "Proto Representations"? The Cognitive Value of Affect-Sharing in Early Interactions', article presented at the World Association of Infant Psychiatry, Cannes, 1983.

Premack, A. J., 'Upgrading a Mind', in T. Bever, J. Carroll, and W. Miller, *Talking Minds* (Cambridge, Mass.: MIT Press, 1984), 181–209.

Rosch, E., and Floyd, B. (eds.), *Cognition and Categorization* (Hillsdale, NJ: Erlbaum, 1978).

RUFF, H. A., 'The Development of Perception and Recognition of Objects', *Child Development*, 51 (1980), 981–92.

SPELKE, E. S., 'The Development of Intermodal Perception', in L. B. Cohen and P. Salapatek (eds.), *Handbook of Infant Perception* (New York: Academic Press, 1982).

MOTHER–CHILD INTERACTION

BATES, E. (ed.), *The Emergence of Symbols: Cognition and Communication in Infancy* (New York: Academic Press, 1979).

BEEBE, B., and SLOATES, P., 'Assessment and Treatment of Difficulties in Mother-Infant Attunement in the First Three Years of Life: A Case History', *Psychoanalytic Inquiry*, 1:4 (1982), 601–23.

BOWER, T. G. R., *Development in Infancy* (San Francisco: W. H. Freeman, 1974).

BOWLBY, J., *Attachment and Loss* (3 vols. London: Hogarth Press, 1969–80).

BURD, A. P., and MILEWSKI, A. E., 'Matching of Facial Gestures by Young Infants: Imitation or Releasers?', article presented at a meeting of the Society for Research in Child Development, Boston, Mass., 1981.

COLLIS, G. M., and SCHAFFER, H. R., 'Synchronisation of Visual Attention in Mother–Infant Pairs', *Journal of Child Psychiatry*, 16 (1975), 315–20.

DeCASPER, A. J., and FIFER, W. P., 'Of Human Bonding: Newborns Prefer their Mother's Voice', *Science*, 208 (1980), 1174–6.

DIATKINE, R., 'L'Autisme infantile précoce: Un point de vue psychanalytique en 1993', *La Psychiatrie de l'enfant*, 36:2 (1993), 363–412.

——and SIMON, J., *La Psychanalyse précoce* (Paris: Presses universitaires de France, 1972).

FIELD, T. M., WOODSON, R., GREENBERG, R., and COHEN, D., 'Discrimination and Imitation of Facial Expressions by Neonates', *Science*, 218 (1982), 179–81.

FREEDMAN, M., and GAND, S. (eds.), *Communicative Structures and Psychic Structures* (New York: Plenum Press, 1977).

LEBOVICI, S., *Le Nourisson, la mère et le psychanalyste: Les Interactions précoces* (Paris: Le Centurion, 1983).

——'La Relation objectale chez l'enfant', *Psychiatrie de l'enfant*, 3:1 (1961), 154–62.

LEWIS, M., and ROSENBLUM, L. (eds.), *The Development of Affect* (New York: Plenum Press, 1978).

MAHLER, MARGARET S. *et al.*, *The Psychological Birth of the Human Infant: Symbiosis and Individuation* (New York: Basic Books, 1975).

STERN, D. N., *Le Monde interpersonnel du nourisson* (Paris: Presses universitaires de France, 1985).

WINNICOTT, D. W., *Through Paediatrics to Psycho-analysis* (London: Hogarth Press, 1974).

——*Playing and Reality* (Harmondsworth: Penguin Books, 1974).

CHILD PSYCHOLOGY

BIDEAUD, J., and HOUDÉ, O., 'Le Développement des catégorisations: Capture logique ou capture écologique des propriétés', *L'Année psychologique* (1989).

PIAGET, J., *La Formation du symbole* (Neuchâtel: Delachaux & Niestlé, 1945).

VYGOTSKY, L. S., *La Pensée et le langage* (Paris: Editions Sociales, 1985).

WALLON, H., *L'Evolution psychologique de l'enfant* (Paris: Armand Colin, 1941).

WERNER, H., and KAPLAN, B., *Symbol Formation: An Organismic-Developmental Approach to Language and Expression of Thought* (New York: Wiley, 1963).

SPEECH DISORDERS

BOREL-MAISONNY, S., 'Les Troubles de la parole', in André Martinet (ed.), *Le Langage*, La Pléiade (Paris: Gallimard, 1973), 369–89.

BRESSON, M. F., 'L'Etat actuel des recherches sur les dysphasies', in *Les Textes du centre Alfred Binet, Dysphasies*, 11 (1987), 25–51.

CARAMAZZA, A., and ZURIF, E. B., *Language Acquisition and Language Breakdown: Parallels and Divergences* (Baltimore: Johns Hopkins University Press, 1978).

CHRISTE, R., CHRISTE-LUTERBACHER, M. M., and LUQUET, P., *La Parole troublée, Le Fait psychanalytique* (Paris: Presses universitaires de France, 1987).

DE AJURIAGUERRA, J., DIATKINE, R., and KALMANSON, D., 'Les Troubles du développement du langage au cours des états psychotiques précoces', *La Psychiatrie de l'enfant*, 2:1 (Paris: Presses universitaires de France, 1959) 1–65.

DIATKINE, R., 'Essai sur les dysphasies', in *Les Textes du centre Alfred Binet, Dysphasies*, 11 (1987), 1–16.

DUCARNE, B., *Rééducation sémiologique de l'aphasie* (Paris: Masson, 1988).

EISENSON, J., *Aphasia in Children* (New York: Harper Row, 1972).

EWING, A. W. G., *Aphasia in Childhood* (Oxford: Oxford University Press, 1930)

FREUD, S., 'Zur Auffassung der Aphasien', *Gesammelte Werke*, 1, (1891), i. English trans.: *On Aphasia* (Imago Publishing, 1953).

FRANÇOIS, F., 'Interprétation linguistique et psychopathologique', *Evolution Psychiatrique*, 49:2 (1984).

GOLDSTEIN, K., 'L'Analyse de l'aphasie et l'étude de l'essence du langage', *Journal de Psychologie*, 30 (1933), 430–96.

GUTMAN, E., 'Aphasia in Children', *Brain*, 65 (1942), 205–19.

HÉCAEN, H., and ANGELERGUES, R., *Pathologie du langage, Langue et langage* (Paris: Larousse, 1965).

HOUZEL, D., Introduction to 'Genèse et psycho-pathologie du langage chez l'enfant', *Neuropsychiatrie de l'enfance et de l'adolescence*, 32:10/11 (Brest, 1983), 477–91.

LIBERMANN, A. M., COOPER, F. S., SHANKWEILER, D. F., and STUDDERT-KENNEDY, M., 'Perception of the Speech Code', *Psychological Review*, 74 (1967), 431–61.

LURIIA, A. R., 'Brain Disorder and Language Analysis', *Language and Speech*, 1 (1958), 14–34.

RAPIN, I., and WILSON, B. C., 'Children with Developmental Language Disability: Neurological Aspects and Assessments', in M. A. Wyke (ed.), *Developmental Dysphasia* (New York: Academic Press, 1978), 13–41.

RONDAL, J., and SÉRON, X., *Troubles du langage, diagnostic et rééducation* (Brussels: Mardarga, 1982).

LANGUAGE IN PSYCHOANALYSIS:
SYMBOLIZATION

ANZIEU, D. *et al.*, *Psychanalyse et langage* (Paris: Dunod, 1977).

DANON-BOILEAU, L., *Le Sujet de l'énonciation* (Paris: Ophrys, 1984).

FREUD, S., *The Interpretation of Dreams* (Harmondsworth: Penguin, 1991).

FREUD, S. *Collected Papers*, ed. J. Riviere (New York: Basic Books, 1959).

GIBEAULT, A., 'Symbolisme primitif et formation des symboles. De l'apport des post-kleiniennes à la théorie de symbolisation', *Nouvelle revue de Psychanalyse*, 26 (1982).

GREEN, A., 'Le langage dans la psychanalyse', in *Langages, Deuxièmes rencontres psychanalytiques d'Aix-en-Provence* (Paris: Les Belles Lettres, 1983), 19–250.

JONES, E., 'The Theory of Symbolism', in *Papers on Psychoanalysis* (London: Ballière & Tindall, 1968).

KLEIN, M., 'The Importance of Symbol-Formation in the Development of the Ego', *International Journal of Psychoanalysis*, 11 (1930).

LUQUET, P., 'Langage, pensée et structure psychique', in *Rapport du 47e congrès des psychanalystes de langue française des pays romans* (1987).

PICHON, E., 'La Grammaire en tant que mode d'exploration de l'inconscient', *L'Evolution Psychiatrique*, 1 (1925), 237–57.

ROSEMBERG, B., 'Sur la négation', *Cahiers du Centre de psychanalyse et de psychotérapie*, 2 (1981).

GENERAL LINGUISTICS

BENVENISTE, E., *Problèmes de linguistique générale* (2 vols.; Paris: Gallimard, 1966; 1974).

BUHLER, K., 1934, *Theory of Language* (Amsterdam/Philadelphia: Benjamins, 1990).

CASSIRER, E., *The Philosophy of Symbolic Forms*, trans. from the German by R. Manheim (New Haven: Yale University Press, 1953–7), i.

CULIOLI, A., *Pour une linguistique de l'énonciation*, Opérations et Représentations (Paris: Ophrys, 1990), i.

Index